AN ACCIDENTAL
GLOBETROTTER

ALSO BY JEFF MARTINDALE

Going to the Beach

Random Thoughts

AN ACCIDENTAL
GLOBETROTTER

A Travel Memoir

By
Jeff Martindale

iUniverse, Inc.
Bloomington

AN ACCIDENTAL GLOBETROTTER
A Travel Memoir

iUniverse books may be ordered through booksellers or by contacting:

iUniverse
1663 Liberty Drive
Bloomington, IN 47403
www.iuniverse.com
1-800-Authors (1-800-288-4677)

ISBN: 978-1-4759-6116-4 (sc)
ISBN: 978-1-4759-6117-1 (ebk)

Library of Congress Control Number: 2012921153

Printed in the United States of America

iUniverse rev. date: 01/28/2013

CONTENTS

Introduction..ix

Chapter 1   Welcome to Europe!.....................................1
Chapter 2   Beer and Brussels..16
Chapter 3   Vive la France!..29
Chapter 4   Spontaneous Germany 58
Chapter 5   Return to the Netherlands.............................74
Chapter 6   Beautiful Belgium 80
Chapter 7   Miscellaneous Observations.........................85
Appendix   Halfway Around the World: India...............89
    Day 1   Departure..89
    Day 2   The First Day in Mumbai 101
    Day 3   All Around the Town..................................105
    Day 4   A Day Off 108
    Day 5   Delhi..113
    Day 6   Light at the End of the Tunnel 118
    Day 7-8   Going Home 121

Author's Note...129
About the Author 131

For Sherry

Loving aunt. Inspiring reader.
Dedicated teacher and principal.

INTRODUCTION

Oh, the joys of air travel!

Okay, maybe "joy" isn't the ideal word to describe modern-day air travel. Frankly, the words "joy" and "air travel" haven't appeared in the same sentence since the Johnson (Lyndon, not Andrew) Administration, unless perhaps a weary traveler mentioned how much *joy* they had once their *air travel* experience mercifully ended. While most air travelers bemoan the draconian cost-cutting and annoying penny-pinching fees employed by U.S. airlines that has relegated a once superb service offering to little more than a glorified air taxi, I, for one, have drawn upon my positive attitude and seemingly boundless naïveté to tolerate air travel as a never-boring means to an end.

As a child, going to the airport occurred so infrequently that my memories are always positive, mainly because it meant embarking on a family vacation. As an adult, I'm fortunate to make only infrequent business trips, and never before had I traveled internationally before the accounts portrayed in this book. I was a nervous wreck leading up to departure day, knowing I would travel so far from home, which was compounded with the dread of today's air travel, which has decayed into a skeleton of its former self.

The stress is often reflected in the expressions of departing passengers. In the good ole days, a wife drove her husband to the airport, perhaps toting his suitcase to the terminal, sending him off with a kiss and long embrace, and waving to him as he disappeared down the jetway.

These days, my wife sends me away with a brief hug and quick kiss from the security of our kitchen. I drive myself to the airport and tote my own bags. While I wait for my flight, I may call her on my cell phone, in between bites of a $10 hamburger purchased from an airport vendor, and say, casually, almost wistfully, "You know, it didn't occur to me to have you drive me to the airport." She responds with a snort before ticking off the myriad of activities on her packed schedule, which means, in no uncertain terms, there's no way in Sam Hill that she could take me to the airport.

Not that I'm complaining, mind you. I'm just making a simple observation.

Additionally, one can't pack for a trip without the ever-present fear of checking an overweight bag and incurring one of the cash-strapped airlines' many surcharges that loom over our wallets like a vulture. It's getting to where everyone is surcharged to death. Surcharges for sitting in an exit row, for changing a reservation, for having more than one piece of checked luggage. It's hard enough to pack for a two-week overseas business trip, but try cramming a 14-day supply of clothes into a single bag and keeping it under the airline's 50-pound weight limit.

Check-in is hardly a breeze unless you fly more than the Wallenda Brothers and accumulate enough frequent flyer miles to qualify for an airline's elite travel program, which allows for speedier check-in, shorter lines at security, and a whole can of soda to consume with a bigger bag of pretzels. Otherwise, remember to pack the latest Stephen King novel in your carry-on bag because you're in for long queues and Methuselah-esque waits with crying babies and slow-moving old ladies dragging oversized bags with cute pink ribbons tied in bows on the handle.

Frequent flyers can insulate themselves inside secure frequent traveler clubs, which are clean and spacious, offering complimentary food and beverages (including a fair selection of beers and booze), comfortable chairs (always plush and padded), free newspapers, fast Wi-Fi, and oversized flat screen televisions.

However, working-class stiffs like yours truly wait in crowded gate areas inconveniently located at the far end of terminals, where hundreds of weary travelers congregate like cattle and invade each other's personal space while awaiting mass simultaneous flight departures at gates clustered closely together.

I remember waiting in the Memphis airport when a woman and her three daughters emerged from the masses and took business class seats to my right. The woman of Middle Eastern descent was tall and elegantly dressed, her head wrapped in black cloth that draped over her shoulders and down her back, covering her hair, leaving only her copper-toned face exposed.

Her daughters were aged roughly nine, six and two, chatterbox bundles of energy, particularly the youngest one, who appeared quite the handful. Her name was Sorrah. I know this because her mother incessantly bellowed her name. We got to know Sorrah very well prior to boarding. For example, Sorrah doesn't like to be told 'no'. She liked to pass the time by whacking her big sisters with whatever was within range, her favorite being a toy that barked an annoying "Pop Goes the Weasel" tune with each blow. Sorrah also disliked sitting next to her mother, preferring instead to squeal—shriek, really—in the middle of the departure gate area, her yelps piercing the din of the crowd.

Sorrah and her family spoke no English but everyone within earshot clearly understood her mother's exasperated tone, familiar to all parents with troublesome kids. I needed no 'Arabic for Dummies' to understand Sorrah's mother's frustrating rebukes in their native tongue, and it meant something like, "Stop it right now, you pint sized bitch!"

Curiosity also made me wonder how "Sorrah" translated to English. I decided it meant "shrieking menace."

It would later be my good fortune to accept a pre-flight request to switch business class seats so a family could sit together. "I figured you wouldn't want to sit next to a bunch of kids," explained the gate agent, pleasantly, and presciently it would turn out, as Sorrah's family reaped the benefit of my generosity, borne in part from the memory of a corporate colleague who, years earlier, blatantly and with great conviction refused to concede his aisle seat for the window seat immediately behind him so a mother and daughter could sit together, this occurring across from me and in the face of the family in question.

I didn't mind switching at all. Traveling is hard enough, even without attending to the needs of children.

Not that the government makes traveling any easier.

Nowadays, even Canada and Mexico require a passport. Mexico, I can understand. It's totally logical that Uncle Sam wants to control the import of illegal immigrants, superior tequila and homegrown marijuana. But Canada? Come on! What's to fear about Canada, except perhaps ice hockey and people that finish their sentences with "eh"? The last I heard, the most popular illegal imports from Canada were cheaper prescription drugs and Cadbury chocolates, but I digress.

As I mentioned earlier, there are few joys more satisfying than reaching the end of a long journey, especially one that takes you to a new destination. The travels depicted in this memoir occurred during a business trip to Europe in September, 2006. The appendix includes bonus material from another business trip to India in October, 2005. It will hopefully inform you on some of the most beautiful, scenic and historic places Europe and India has to offer. Perhaps my experiences will enlighten and humor you, for I firmly believe that we should experience this wonderful world as much as possible, and do so with a smile.

CHAPTER 1

Welcome to Europe!

As Westerners approach Amsterdam from the west, the view suddenly transforms from expansive, monotonous ocean to scenic, bucolic landscapes. Descending through gunmetal gray skies and billowy clouds threatening rain, I gazed out the window and watched the North Sea morph into the Netherlands coast, first a narrow strip of beach followed by a lush green undulating landscape dotted by tiny houses with slate roofs.

Amsterdam, called "the greatest planned city of northern Europe" in one article, has always been one of the world's most well-known cities. Way back in the 17th Century, Amsterdam was arguably the center of the world's economy, though today it appears to be most widely-known for its liberal, open-minded policies (much more on that later).

Amsterdam was founded as a fishing village around the 13th Century. The city developed around a dam in the Amstel River, hence the name, written in the early days as "Amstelledamme". Amsterdam is sometimes called "the Venice of the North", and one need only review a city map to understand why.

Canals are ever-present in Amsterdam, radiating like concentric circles around a central hub which is the Central Station. All roads seem to lead to the Central Station and a city map resembles a hub and spoke system, with the Central Station being the transportation axis around which this planned city revolves.

Amsterdam reportedly has 165 canals, 1,281 bridges, 70 cruise boats, 8 wooden drawbridges, 2,500 houseboats and 120 water bikes. It's common for people to live in houseboats tethered to the banks of the canal, and everywhere there are small boats parallel parked like cars along the canal edge. Slowly churning their way through the brown canal waters, cruise boats, gorged with tourists snapping photos of the town's historic beauty, are a common sight.

One should experience the canals in the safety of canal boats because the water is brown for a reason, and it has nothing to do with sediment, unless "sediment" is the by-product of natural processes by which houseboat residents expel unwanted solids and liquids from their persons. I'd sooner chew on a razor blade than, say, go swimming in an Amsterdam canal.

Twice I've visited Amsterdam, for a total of two days, but I could have easily spent weeks exploring its charming beauty. While Amsterdam is large city—population about one million—located in the Netherlands (also known as Holland), it doesn't "feel" like a big city, more like Nashville than the New York-feel of more popular European destinations like Paris, London or Rome.

Getting around Amsterdam is quite easy, either by foot, bike or its extensive public transportation system, which I initially dreaded due to inexperience and language concerns, but soon discovered its accessibility and user friendliness.

I'd read about the Europeans' extensive use of public transportation, but was quite apprehensive about how well I'd navigate the logistics of European mass transit, my primary hang-up an inability to speak the local language. Fortunately, I resisted the macho urge to figure it out on my own and humbly asked for help when necessary, which was often.

The first step involved buying a train ticket to the nearest tram station, at which point I would buy another ticket to a tram stop near my hotel. The purchase transacted rather simply, though not without some loss in the translation, as I must have poorly enunciated my question for the ticket agent—a butch-looking, middle-aged lady whose closely-cropped Annie Lennox-style hairdo could've easily passed her off as a man, because her expression bespoke confusion if not outright disdain ("Ze dumb American!"). But I eventually got my point across and she sold me a train ticket for 3€ and directed me to the proper platform, though I first detoured by an information desk because I didn't understand the agent's thick accent from which of twelve platforms my train departed.

I descended a long escalator and, after a short wait, boarded a train, my destination being the World Trade Center station, the first stop after Schiphol (sounds like "SKIP-pull") International Airport. The train emerged from an underground tunnel to an elevated rail splitting a bustling expressway, its cars more compact than those in America.

I departed the train and, after wandering the open-air station for a few minutes trying to determine how to buy a tram ticket, I reluctantly cast aside my ego and again asked for help, a friendly local instructing me how to use a ticket kiosk near escalators leading to the tram platform. Inputting 6.70€ bought me 15 full fare strip tickets which could be used for travel on any of the cities buses, trams or metro rail trains. I then calculated how many zones I must cross to reach my destination, which would dictate the appropriate number of tickets to validate.

I waited twenty-five minutes for the tram, which afforded an opportunity to catch my breath, relieved the worst part of my half day's travel was behind me (and, as is often the case when I build something up in my mind to be bigger than it is, it wasn't as bad as I expected). It was standing-room only on the tram, which would've been awkward with my oversized luggage, but, fortunately, it was only a short ride to my destination. I exited at the requisite stop and toted my bags three blocks to my hotel, a Hilton deep in the heart of Amsterdam.

I found a pleasant but smallish room, facing one of Amsterdam's many canals snaking through the city. While perusing the hotel brochure, I learned that John Lennon and Yoko Ono selected a room in this hotel as the site for a peaceful protest in 1969.

Shortly thereafter I changed into more comfortable clothes and set out to see Amsterdam, which, in some respects, was out of character for me. I'm not the most adventurous spirit that ever lived. I'm not talking about the running-a-marathon kind of adventure, but the fly-halfway-around-the-world-and-fend-for-myself-alone-in-a-strange-European-city-where-English-isn't-the-primary-language-and-they-don't-serve-country-fried-steak-and-mashed-potatoes   kind of adventure. Nevertheless, I was undeterred as I left the relative comfort of my hotel, a city map wedged in my back pocket, knowing only I was headed north.

Amsterdam's charm was immediate. The hotel was situated on a narrow, tree-lined cobblestone brick street, split by a well-manicured median shaded by a canopy of tall trees. Nearby residential neighborhoods teemed with brownstone homes set close to the road.

A walking tour is the best way to see Amsterdam, but I learned quickly the importance of keeping my head on a swivel because there are many ways in which pedestrians could be hurt, and not just from the auto traffic.

Bicycles were arguably the primary means of navigating Amsterdam. Nearly half of all traffic movements in the city were by bike. Amsterdam was a biking culture and bike paths lined every road and connected every part of the city. Amsterdamans—Amsterdamians? Amsterdamites? Whatever—the people of Amsterdam really loved their bikes.

Bike lanes were express roads where bikers ruled (and don't wear helmets). The lanes were clearly marked and God-forbid the distracted tourist who ambled into the path. The familiar 'ding' of bicycle bells was an effective warning system to alert tourists and others to get the hell out of the way. If you wanted to drive a local mad, stand in a bike lane and chat or look at a map.

However, one must also lookout for public transportation. As I mentioned, Amsterdam had a very developed and efficient public transportation system, and its many trams and buses competed with compact cars on the crowded city streets. When crossing a road, a pedestrian must cross not only a car lane and bike lane but also a tram lane (think of a tram as a modern, sleek trolley, but not a cable car). Hence, the importance of keeping one's head on a swivel, yielding to bell-ringing bikers, speeding Audis and BMWs and silent trams that could sneak up and flatten you in a second.

Fortunately, I'd learned this in my pre-trip readings so I adeptly kept to the sidewalk and looked both ways twice before crossing a road.

The first destination on my walking tour was the Rijksmuseum. The Rijks (rhymes with 'bikes') was the country's national museum and the largest in the Netherlands, in terms of square footage and the size of its collections. It welcomed more than a million visitors every year.

I'm not an art aficionado—unless the definition of 'art' can be extended to include the Sports Illustrated swimsuit edition—but my hotel room came with a complimentary admission ticket, so I figured, "Why not". Less than a mile from my hotel, the Rijksmuseum anchored one end of a grassy mall called the Museumplein, which also featured the Van Gogh Museum, which apparently didn't offer free tickets to area hotel guests, so I passed on visiting.

Fortunately, my walk to the Rijks was short. It was hard enough navigating a large foreign city with Dutch street signs mounted high on building corners; distinctive royal blue placards with bold-faced white lettering easily viewed once you knew where to look.

Getting directions wasn't as simple as, "Go down Poplar. Take a left on Union. Then right on Madison." These were actual directions to the Rijksmuseum from my hotel:

- Turn left onto Breitnerstraat. Go 0.1 mile.
- Breitnerstraat becomes Cornelius Schuystraat.
- Turn right onto De Lairessestraat. Go 0.3 miles.
- Turn left onto Van Baerlestraat. Go 0.2 miles.
- Turn right onto Jan Luijkenstraat. Go 0.2 miles.

Dutch wasn't an "intuitive" language, all consonants and guttural sounding, like my grandfather hocking up a wad of phlegm. But it wasn't difficult to find the Rijksmuseum.

Approaching the museum's flank, I was intrigued by large white tents—steepled and resembling inverted funnels—arranged in a ring around an ornate fountain and wading pool. Booming speakers blared techno beats of Euro-dance music, which grew louder with each step. The pleasing aroma of hot food tempted my olfactory senses, and I soon wandered into a fine-dining culinary festival.

I hadn't eaten since consuming a bite-sized croissant on the plane hours earlier, so my taste buds salivated like Pavlov's dog. Unfortunately, after a few minutes of strolling between tents, I found no options appealing to my finicky tastes (my diet can be effectively summed up by two words: "meat" and "potatoes").

So, I eschewed the scrumptious smells of the culinary festival and maneuvered through a maze of haphazardly parked bicycles to the Rijksmuseum ingang—'entrance' in Dutch—where, to my tummy's pleasant surprise, a hot dog stand ("Real American Hot Dogs") watched over the main gate. I eagerly forked over 4€ for a steaming hot dog and Coca-Cola (I needed caffeine the way Paris Hilton needed a daily porterhouse).

I devoured the wiener and gulped the soda in the shade of a gothic concrete arch guarding the entrance. Dozens of cooing pigeons rested on the ledge overhead, and I silently hoped that one wouldn't use me for target practice (they didn't).

Once sated, I used the fast lane for pre-paid ticket holders and bypassed a long line of tourists waiting to buy tickets, soon entering the museum.

I must admit that I arrived with a skeptical attitude. Not being a patron of the arts, I expected to breeze through the museum, perhaps pausing on occasion to admire a Rembrandt, soon to continue my Amsterdam exploration, sights set on the tourist site I *really* wanted to see: the Anne Frank House. Surprisingly, though, I found the Rijksmuseum to be quite fascinating.

Most of the building was closed for renovations, but the very best of the Rijks collection was on display in a redesigned wing, in an exhibition called "The Masterpieces", featuring many Rembrandt works, as I happened there during the 400th anniversary of Rembrandt's birthday. The Rijks had rolled out much of its world-famous Rembrandt collection, one of the largest in the world.

I navigated ante rooms displaying a wide variety of delicate pottery, fine sculptures, and ornate doll houses, soon to be captivated by Rembrandt's 17th Century paintings—mostly oils on canvas—as well as others by his protégés and contemporaries.

I was thoroughly impressed by the exquisite paintings and extraordinary detail; many so realistic to resemble photographs. "The Night Watch" is arguably Rembrandt's most famous painting, and its roughly 10-foot square canvas was on display at the end of the exhibition.

One of my favorites, though, was a painting of the prophet Jeremiah, a somber work showing him lamenting the destruction of Jerusalem. Religious imagery was a major theme in works of that era. Another ante room featured Rembrandt's pencil drawings, most of which depicted historical events—episodes from the Bible, classical mythology and the ancient world—supposedly the highest forms of art, so I read.

A museum handout stated Rembrandt had studied the Bible and other texts to tell the story of his drawings more effectively and to empathize with the characters. Biblical scenes were reflected in many of his works. The pencil drawings, for instance, included familiar events as the washing of the disciples' feet, Judas returning pieces of silver, the weeping Marys at Jesus' entombment, and Christ placing his hand on the leper's head, to name a few. Rembrandt—whose full name, I learned, was Rembrandt Harmensz van Rijn—may or may not have been a spiritual man, but he used the Bible as a means for creative inspiration.

Whatever the case may be, I found it an inescapable conclusion that Rembrandt was indeed Holland's greatest 17th Century painter.

I emerged from the Rijks under foreboding skies which had considerably darkened. Slight drizzle misted in the air. I wore a logo-covered road race T-shirt over blue shorts, dressed appropriately for the temperature—about 70 degrees, though it felt slightly cooler with a steady breeze blowing off the North Sea. Faced with a two-mile walk to the Anne Frank House, I could tolerate a mild drizzle but not a steady shower.

I traversed the Leidseplein entertainment district (not to be confused with the Red Light District), a compact development swarming with tourists partaking in the revelry of spirited bars, diverse restaurants (including familiar American chains), and lively entertainment venues. The rain began to fall harder, so I paused under the protective cover of a shop's awning, a special chess match in progress nearby.

About eight feet square, a black-and-white chessboard had been painted on the stone plaza. Two men stood at the board's edge in pensive thought. After a few minutes, one walked onto the board and moved a chess piece the size of a five gallon bucket, dropping it to the plaza floor with a plasticated 'thump'. A goodly crowd had formed, watching the action—or lack of it, depending on your knowledge of the game, of which I had little—some offering advice, others snapping pictures. When the rain eased up, I went on my way.

Twenty minutes later, I reached the Anne Frank House, where I found a long line of tourists stretched around a corner of the building. I assumed a position at the end of the queue and waited.

The Anne Frank House isn't the house where she grew up but is instead the building where her father owned a business and she lived in hiding with her family when the Nazis occupied Amsterdam and began persecuting the Jews during World War II. For more than two years, Anne Frank lived in its annex with another family, and was the place immortalized in her diaries, now a treasure of world literature.

Anne Frank and her family fled to The Netherlands in 1933 when Hitler rose to power in Germany. In May 1940, German Nazis occupied The Netherlands, increasing their repression of Jews there as well. The Frank family went into hiding in this building on July 6, 1942.

The building was comprised of two sections: the front part of the house and a back part—referred to as the annex. Anne Frank's father, Otto, ran a company in the front part, with offices and storerooms and a warehouse running the length of the building, extending under the annex out back. Eight people lived in hiding in the rear upper floors for more than two years before being betrayed and discovered only months before Amsterdam's liberation by the Allies.

The house was a place of history and reverence; photograph taking and cell phone usage being strictly forbidden. A gentleman in front of me answered his cell phone inside the building just as he was passing a security guard, who immediately threw open an exit door and told him—sternly but kindly—to finish his call outside, then he would gladly allow him reentry.

I toured the house slowly and silently, reviewing the many exhibits, pausing to watch the occasional video featuring survivors from the Anne Frank story. Walking through the storefront was thought-provoking, but nothing compared to the power and awe of witnessing the famous landing with the movable bookcase that concealed the entrance to the annex.

The doorway to the secret annex was concealed behind a movable bookcase constructed especially for this purpose. Seeing it in person was almost surreal. It was kept open now as one must walk around it to enter the secret annex, which required the navigation of a steep step and simultaneously ducking one's head.

The stairs in the annex were nearly vertical and had to be navigated carefully. Once in the annex, the steady procession of tourists ambled in silence, respectful of the site's historical significance, the shuffling of feet the only sound breaking the reverent peace.

In Anne's parents' room, a map of Normandy tacked to the wall marked where Otto followed the Allied Forces advancing during the war. Next to it were dated pencil ticks tracking Anne's and her sister's growth during the hiding period.

Anne's room was a small, narrow space which she shared with a man named Fritz Pheffer. The desk where she penned her now-famous diary lined the corner of one wall. She tacked to the same wall photos and miscellaneous items—photos of entertainers clipped from the newspaper, pictures of the Dutch Royal Family and Princess (now Queen) Elizabeth of England—in an attempt to liven up the drab surroundings. An advertisement for Opetka—Otto Frank's company—hung by the window.

The bathroom contained a tiny water closet and decorative blue-and-white porcelain toilet, which, with the sink, could only be used outside of regular office hours because the water and drainage pipes ran through a wall in the warehouse. It was crucial to everyone's safety that the warehousemen didn't discover them hiding in the Secret Annex.

In perhaps the most powerful moment of the tour, I entered a small museum that housed under protective glass the original Anne Frank diaries—three of them total. The first display case held Anne's first diary, which she received on her thirteenth birthday. Once she filled this diary, Anne continued writing in school exercise notebooks. She later edited and reworked her diary on loose sheets of paper.

Anne Frank dreamed about publishing a "novel about the Secret Annex" based on her original diary texts. Little did she know the extent to which the world would know her poignant and insightful writings that belied her age.

The Diary of Anne Frank should be required reading for all people, if for no other reason than to enlighten everyone about the prejudice, discrimination, and human rights abuses that marked the era and continue still today. It's an inspiring piece of literature, written in a style so profound and insightful that it's hard to believe the author was only fourteen. I read it years ago but think I will read it again. Having seen the Secret Annex with my own eyes, I was very moved by the experience.

Upon leaving the Anne Frank House, I set a course for the remaining attraction on my agenda: the Red Light District. It didn't escape me that perhaps I should've visited them in reverse order, for it felt anticlimactic—if not a bit sacrilegious—to visit the sites in the order I chose, but I expected not to be so stirred at the Secret Annex.

Anyhow, a short ten-minute walk separated me from Amsterdam's most notorious tourist attraction, which I found to be at once graphic and fascinating.

The Red Light District left little to the imagination. Sex shops. Sex museums. Peep shows with private viewing booths. Straight bars. Gay bars. Private brothels, where "a more traditional form of prostitution" was practiced. Live sex shows (one bar—the de Bananenbar—encouraged "audience participation" for its interactive sex shows featuring bananas). It was definitely an in-your-face place.

The district received its name from the red neon-fringed window parlors, where women in various stages of undress displayed their goods, so to speak. Many of the windows were vacant given the afternoon hour, but there was no shortage of "eye candy", the packs of men parading the streets could pause at regular intervals to look at—but not take pictures of (that's a big no-no)—their wildest wet dreams in the flesh, separated by a simple glass door, the thinnest of margins—literally and morally.

Discussions about price occurred in the open doorways. I could only imagine how that discussion might begin ("Hi, how much for the coitus / fellatio combo?"). There were dozens, if not hundreds, of women ready and willing to separate a man from his money—not to mention his sperm—every fantasy fulfilled for a pocketful of euros, though the lack of Visa and MasterCard stickers on the windows left it unclear whether they accepted credit cards.

The window parlors were little more than glorified closets, booths glowing in red neon, sparsely decorated save for a small bed, where the "tricks" took place. These women were salespeople, and could often be found tapping on windows as you passed by, inviting you to approach with curled fingers, sexy come-hither looks, and, in one instance, a black vibrator the size of my arm with a baseball-sized tip that seemed to defy conventional usage.

Prostitution was legal in Holland, officially since late 2000 but unofficially for centuries. Legalizing the world's oldest profession allowed the government to ensure all prostitutes could access medical care and work in better conditions by regulating and monitoring working practices and standards. In short, prostitutes were taxpayers.

The city of Amsterdam took pride in its liberal attitudes toward sex and drugs. One article I read stated that Amsterdam "embrac(es) the fact that people may be into prostitution, soft drugs, and pornography—and this is only human. So instead of criminalizing everything, this very upfront city wears its heart on its sleeve—what you see is what you get."

Well, from what I could tell, one could pretty much get whatever he wanted in Amsterdam. No vice went unsatisfied. If you couldn't find it there, it can't be found.

Another thing one could find without looking very hard was copious amounts of marijuana. Countless coffeehouses dotted the landscape, on the main avenues and shadowy side alleys (some so narrow that it was impossible to fully extend your arms away from your body). Coffeehouses sold small amounts of cannabis (less than 5 grams), where one ordered from overhead menus the same way you might order a Subway sandwich. Its sale was strictly regulated—that is, the marijuana, not club sandwiches—and, like the sex parlors, taxed. It didn't take long after entering the district to detect the tell-tale pungent aroma, which permeated the air like oxygen.

It was illegal to smoke marijuana in public, which I assumed to mean on street corners or standing in a public plaza, but lawbreakers usually got off—no pun intended—with a reminder from the authorities. My pre-trip reading contained the following bit of advice: "It is not polite either to roam the streets, shops or restaurants while stoned. You can easily bump into a bike or a tram and die."

Given the pervasiveness of casual drug use, I half expected to be overrun by stoned tourists and locals. However, only a few candidates fit the bill, most notably a fifty-something man with glazed eyes and tousled hair, existing in body but not mind, staggering through an alley as though someone tilted the world beneath his feet, a six-inch string of saliva dangling from his mouth.

I was tempted to follow to see if he would become tram-kill, but hunger pangs distracted me and I continued on my way.

Despite the preponderance of drugs and blatant sexual indulgence, the Red Light District was actually a beautiful section of Amsterdam. It had scenic tree-lined canals, charming and authentic restaurants, and narrow cobblestone streets. One article I read described its "utterly charming 14th Century architecture", such as the gothic Oude Kerk, or Old Church, that set in the center of it all ("utterly" being a descriptive term and in no way related to the ever-present mammaries on display).

At no point did I feel threatened by my surroundings as clusters of police and thousands of sightseers milled about. I understood the area was once a shadowy and seedy part of town ('seedy' being a relative term, I guess) but I found it to be clean and charming in its own way.

As the clock approached seven, the sun slowly disappeared below the horizon, and my energy level similarly sank. I wandered the streets and alleys for a half-hour seeking a suitable restaurant, determined to stifle my culinary inhibitions and partake in the local cuisine, but the best option—a Greek gyro café—offered more greasy fare than my stomach desired. So I concluded my nearly five-hour walking tour, boarded a southbound tram and returned to the hotel, dining instead in the hotel's Italian restaurant, where I ate a scrumptious but brief dinner—'brief' referring to the incredulous looks offered by my Italian waiter. He seemed not to understand why I desired a fleeting dining experience, so quickly dismissing the wine list for bottled water, refusing even to review the dessert menu in favor of returning to my room, which I did directly after signing the check. In his defense, he couldn't have known that I suffered from jet lag, but in my defense, I hadn't yet discovered how Europeans truly savor a dining experience.

5:15 a.m. Sunday morning. I pulled back the curtains to find more of the same lead-gray skies that greeted me the prior day. Rainwater pooled on the rooftop beneath my window and a stiff pre-dawn breeze ruffled the treetops, which tilted in the direction of the wind. Uncertain whether or not to brave the elements for a run in a nearby park, I cemented the decision after watching a half-hour of mind-numbing hotel television, the most engaging broadcast being a Crepflo A. Dollar sermon on one of the few English-speaking stations worth watching outside the boring BBC channels.

I laced up my new running shoes—sufficiently broken in by the prior day's walking tour—and descended the lift—the elevator—to the ground floor, but not after a few impatient moments trying to figure out why the lift wouldn't budge. You'd think it'd be intuitive to designate the ground floor as the first floor. But I'd forgotten that hotels in most countries outside the U.S. denote the ground floor with a zero and the 1st floor—actually the second floor (my floor)—with a one. A co-worker once said to consider the 2nd floor as "the 1st floor above the ground floor", but I guess I didn't listen very well.

I asked a doorman manning the 'ingang' to point me in the direction of Vondelpark. He gestured toward a side street, which would lead me to my desired destination.

Vondelpark was the largest park in Amsterdam, and reportedly the most famous park in the country, with about ten million annual visitors. The park was opened to the public in 1865 and on most days the park teemed with dog-walkers, joggers, and families enjoying the play areas and open spaces, but the early hour and questionable weather meant I had the park mostly to myself.

I exited the hotel and, rounding a corner, turned directly into a headwind. Cool temperatures prevailed—I guessed in the low sixties—though it felt much cooler with the wind gusting in my face. The doorman instructed me to follow the road north until I reached the park, and I found it easily after a half-mile of warm-up jogging.

I trailed a jogger on my first lap around the park, for he seemed to know where he was going and I wanted to ensure that I didn't make an inadvertent turn. I ran mostly on the unpaved paths, which ran parallel to serene, winding roads. The scene was idyllic: fog hovered above the inky surface of tranquil lakes surrounded by expansive, dewy lawns, beneath shaded canopies of old growth trees, where rainwater dripped steadily, pooling on the saturated ground. The only noise besides the wind-swept trees was the steady thumping of my footfalls on the sandy trail.

I'd planned to run two laps, which I understood to be 12 kilometers, or a little over seven miles, but I knew after the first 18-minute lap that there was no frickin' way one lap could be six kilometers. For me to run three and a half miles that fast required a five-minute mile pace, which I could accomplish only with a jetpack and roller skates. So, calculating that one lap equaled about two miles, I resigned myself to a third lap to complete my desired distance.

On the second lap, I ran a half-mile fartlek (which is a speed workout and only phonetically resembled expelling unwanted gasses from the body—one of my many talents, according to my family. They joked that my Indian name would be "Farts a Lot"). I picked up the pace and, within a quarter mile, had succeeded in an ego-driven quest to overtake the gentleman who paced my first lap. Feeling strong, I continued the fartlek for a full lap, satisfied with finishing two minutes faster than lap one. However, I'd expended my desire to run in the park, foregoing a third lap for new scenery.

I exited the park and jogged through an upscale neighborhood bordering the park's southern boundary, lights flickering on behind curtained windows as the city came to life. The drizzle evolved into a steady rain as I crossed a major thoroughfare, heading toward the Museumplein. I ran a lap around the deserted mall and zig-zagged through a neighborhood of townhouses before returning to my hotel, where I entered the lobby, sufficiently soaked, dripping a mixture of sweat and rain on the white marble floor.

After showering, I spent the remaining hours packing, and I checked out with ample time remaining before my flight to Brussels.

On the return trip to the airport, I felt like a seasoned traveler, confidently boarding a tram near the hotel, offering my strip ticket to the driver for proper validation, and pressing a halt button on the wall to alert the driver to stop at my desired station. Once there, I self-assuredly approached the ticket window and requested a one-way ticket to the airport. The train arrived a few minutes thereafter and I struggled aboard, dragging my nearly fifty-pound suitcase behind me, a weighty briefcase slung over my shoulder.

I hoped the rest of my European trip would improve, logistically speaking. It was hard enough stifling my insecurities and navigating unfamiliar foreign cities—not to mention toting what my back thought was luggage for three. Once I checked-in at the Amsterdam airport—easily navigated with its ample signage in multiple languages, I eagerly anticipated wasting away the hours in the KLM Crown Room, exploiting its relaxed, roomy setting, ample food options, and plentiful Heineken drafts.

It may not have been much to look forward to, but sometimes even the little blessings mean a lot.

*Amsterdam's famous Rijksmuseum, the national museum
of the Netherlands.*

*Life-sized chess board in Amsterdam's Leidseplein
entertainment district.*

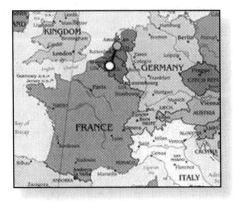

CHAPTER 2

Beer and Brussels

Leaving the excesses of Amsterdam for Brussels, the richly historic capital of Belgium, is, to draw an American comparison, like leaving Las Vegas for Washington, D.C., which is no insult to those Brusselites—Brusselians, whatever—who balk at the comparison to D.C.'s high crime reputation. Frankly, I wouldn't compare my hometown to D.C. either, but it is a cool place to visit ('visit' being the operative word).

Brussels is a mere hour flight from Amsterdam; a flight so short that we began our descent without seemingly finishing our ascent, which gave me just enough time to consume a small bag of pretzels and even smaller orange juice cup—the plastic kind with a peel away lid—hurriedly distributed by the flight attendants. Our flight transpired without incident—just the way I like it—but it didn't escape my attention that our aircraft—a KLM "Cityhopper" Fokker 50, a turbo-prop airliner—showed its age more than Mickey Rooney. It creaked and moaned like my grandfather's knees, so I tried not to think about it, which is to say I failed miserably.

We arrived on time, deplaned, and walked what seemed like miles to baggage claim, though the journey wasn't entirely unpleasant.

European airports are airy and inviting, modern architecture with exposed trusses and glass windows allowing natural light to illuminate wide, clean concourses. Perhaps some modern American airports fit this description—Reagan Airport in D.C. and Detroit come to mind—but there was no real comparison to the aesthetically-pleasing appearances of European airports, at least those that I saw.

Anyhow, the hike to baggage claim, while lengthy, offered the benefit that our bags revolved on the carousel as we approached. We hailed a taxi, which carried us to our hotel—the Scandic Grand Palace, in the heart of downtown Brussels.

Brussels is the capital city of Belgium and the center of many EU institutions. Its metropolitan area counted about two million residents with two primary areas, or regions: French (in the south and city center) and Flemish, or Dutch (in the north). The city was officially bilingual but most of its residents spoke French.

Reading about the city's history, I learned that its founding dates to 979 AD when Charles, the banished son of King Louis IV of France, is said to have built a small castle on an island in the Senne River. Today, Brussels—or Bruxelles in French—was a large modern city that played an important role in European politics but hadn't lost its historic charm.

My hotel was situated on a narrow, hilly cobbled avenue in the central business district. Upon checking in, Gopal and our manager, Ann, who accompanied me from Amsterdam, desired some down time due to exhaustion from their intercontinental travels, and we agreed to meet three hours hence for dinner. I stayed in my room long enough to drop off my bag, place a few calls, and use the WC (the 'water closet', as the toilet was often called), before venturing into the city.

Located one block up the hill—the Treurenberg Hill—from our hotel was an incredibly beautiful Gothic cathedral—the Cathedral of St. Michael and St. Gudula. Thinking the church closed due to the late hour, I'd planned to pause only long enough to snap a few pics of the exterior, but I noticed people streaming out an open front door so I went inside.

I had never in my life seen a church so beautiful.

The building oozed history, dating to the beginning of the 13th Century and required nearly 300 years of construction. Many incredible features competed for my attention. Side aisles overlooked by vibrant 19th

Century stained glass windows. 17th Century confessional boxes carved in oak. Baroque-style statues of the apostles hung from the columns in the nave. Mausoleum crypts—some dating to the 1600s—covered by large marble slabs rose from the floor. A high alter gilded in copper. Side chapels guarded by polished statues. A 'great organ' with 4,300 pipes, 63 stops, 4 keyboards and the pedal-board mounted in a "bird's nest" position high above the cathedral floor. Holes cut in the floor—covered by thick Plexiglass—revealed excavations of the original 13th Century foundations.

Due to its central location in the country's capital city, the cathedral was often used for prominent Catholic ceremonies, including royal marriages and state funerals.

I strolled around the church for half an hour, impressed, absorbing everything, pausing on occasion in worshipful silence, even lighting a candle in honor of Lana and the boys.

I emerged from the church, the skies still cloudy and muted grey, and noticed a distinctive spire rising above the building tops. With ninety minutes to kill before meeting my colleagues for dinner, I set out in that direction.

After a three block walk, I arrived in a plaza surrounded by fascinatingly ornate buildings, a center square packed with thousands of people enjoying a festival of some sort, dozens of steepled tents arranged in two rows and surrounded by a ring of metal barricades. A banner draped above the celebration announced I had stumbled into a the final day of a three-day beer fest, smack dab in the middle of the Grand Place, the central market square of Brussels, its most distinctive tourist destination, and arguably the most fascinating town center in Europe.

It was an extraordinary town square; the most distinctive and dominant building being the Town Hall, constructed in the early 15th Century. Other buildings included guild houses (one of which, Le Swan, served as the home for Karl Marx when he wrote his famous *Manifesto)*, elegant hotels, and inviting restaurants with sidewalk seating.

I wandered around the square, admiring the beautiful buildings, watching people. A sign announced free admission to the beer fest, but one needed three euros to buy beer tickets. Never one to forego a festive occasion where beer is served—or, better yet, a festive occasion with beer as the guest of honor—I quickly found a ticket line, eagerly dug euro coins from my pocket, and received in exchange four Belgian Beer bottle caps.

Surmising that the bottle caps were my "beer tickets", I crossed the threshold into the barricaded area, threaded through the mob of partygoers, my radar on high alert for a suitable brew. A small billboard at one end of the plaza listed an extensive menu, about 200 total offerings, none of which contained the words "Budweiser" or "Miller", which was probably a good thing.

Brewers served their beers in distinctive logo glasses, which made identifying potential candidates easier by the names branded on them. I quickly eliminated anything colored black or dark brown, my aversion to dark beers rooted in my first Guinness experience.

In St. Louis for my younger brother's law school graduation, my grandfather and I wandered the wide passageways of the St. Louis Union Station mall, his eyes lighting up at first sight of a neon 'Guinness' sign illuminating the window of an Irish pub.

"C'mon, Jeff," he bellowed. "I'll buy you a beer."

He promptly ordered two Guinness drafts and handed one to me. I'd never consumed a Guinness beer, and for good reason, preferring to give wide berth to drinks that resembled something drained from my car engine every 3,000 miles. Plus, its two-inch thick head reminded me of Cujo's frothing.

Indifferent to my unease, my grandfather—who liked drinking warm PBR beer, a disconcerting omen, I admit—eagerly savored his beer. Meanwhile, I considered mine with the enthusiasm I would bring to a hernia exam.

"Ugh!" I groaned after the first sip. "I don't like this, Papa."

His eyes shot open. "You don't like it?"

I shook my head, holding the glass at arms length like a dirty diaper.

"You can have it," I replied, setting my glass next to him at the bar.

He promptly downed his glass, then mine.

I've never since consumed a Guinness beer, or anything remotely resembling one.

Bypassing the obviously dark and colored beers—red beer appeared to be a popular choice—I settled on two amber lagers: one called Palm Royale and another, my favorite, called Maes (sounds like "moss").

I lingered over an hour in the Grand Place (sounds like "grahnd ploss", not 'grayand playce' like my Southern accent must've sounded to the locals), sipping unfamiliar but tasty Belgian beers, entertained by a brass band playing folk songs to the merriment of the revelers, who sang along and clapped to the beat. If it hadn't been for a casual glance at someone's watch—I can sum up in two words why I stopped wearing one in 1997: poison ivy—I would've missed meeting my colleagues for dinner.

Suitably buzzed, I strode double time to the hotel, finding Gopal in the lobby as I pushed open the double glass doors. Ann descended the elevator shortly thereafter, and we embarked on our dinner mission.

We walked through and around the Grahnd Ploss for close to an hour, surveying menus posted on entrance windows and handwritten on chalkboards, unable to find suitable vegetarian options for Gopal, not that the choices were few. An abundance of restaurants lined the narrow alleys radiating from the main square, their colorful awnings nearly kissing overhead, the proprietors standing out front, encouraging passers-by to stop in, some more enthusiastically—and confrontationally—than others (One even made a pass at Ann!). We ultimately settled on a Greek restaurant, small and quaint with only ten tables, its exposed rafters painted black, which contrasted nicely with white-painted stone walls.

I savored a scrumptious meal—a delicious scampi dish in a creamy red sauce—at a corner table beneath threads of world currency—dollars, euros, rupees, rials, etc.—strung over our heads and taped to the molding above the bar. Near the end of our dinner, two men emerged from the back, one playing a guitar, the other strumming a small harp, and they regaled everyone with Greek music and song.

Following dinner, everyone's sweet tooth craved dessert, so we returned to the Grahnd Ploss, having earlier spotted a café that would fit the bill. It had rained during dinnertime, so the sidewalk tables sat mostly empty, save for a few sheltered under the protective shell of its russet awning. A waiter scampered out and wiped rainwater from the table as we approached.

Ann and Gopal ordered espresso; I chose hot chocolate. For dessert, Gopal ordered a slice of fruity pie topped with white chocolate shavings. Ann and I, however, ordered what was perhaps the best dessert in Brussels: a Belgian waffle so light and heavenly it would've floated away in the evening breeze if not for the mound of whipped cream and abundance of chocolate sauce weighting it down.

The end of the evening upon us, we strolled to the hotel and addressed some housekeeping details (e.g., ironing wrinkled shirts, sending emails, checking the baseball scores—okay, only I did that) before turning in for the night a little after midnight, silently hoping to avoid dreams about warm Guinness beer.

I awoke early the next morning to find more of the same gloomy, overcast skies that had followed me throughout Europe, though I hadn't required the sun to have a sunny disposition.

After three days in Europe, I finally slept until my alarm sounded, aided by blackout drapes holding the daylight at bay. It was an interesting room, small but clean, which describes many things in Europe—the countries, the cars, the lifts, the beds, the people (fat people in Europe are about as common as skinny people in Tennessee). Speaking of the beds, mine, at first glance, looked full-sized but a closer examination revealed it was actually two twins pushed together, each with a thin but cushiony mattress pad—not a full mattress—atop a box spring, a spread folded with precise hospital corners flush with the edge of the bed (the work of someone who cared about the finer details, no?).

I met Ann and Gopal in the lobby, where we ate a fine breakfast in the hotel 'brasserie', which sounded like a woman's undergarment but meant 'coffeehouse' in French.

Later that day, several Brussels colleagues accompanied us on a pleasant lunch at a nearby Italian restaurant, quaint and charming like the Greek restaurant from the prior evening. After we took a table near the front window, a stubble-faced waiter approached and gestured to a postcard-sized chalkboard resting at the end of the table, divulging in French the day's specialties with the enthusiasm of a man dreading a colonoscopy.

He turned on his heels and strode away and I was no closer to grasping his words than I was to knowing the inner workings of the Space Shuttle.

"Did you understand what he said?" one of the Brussels ladies asked me, observing my blank expression.

"Not a word," I replied. "It sounded like a bunch of gibberish."

Everyone at the table laughed, particularly the Europeans.

I recognized 'ravioli' on the specials board, and a calzone on the menu looked like a possibility, but I chose the former, filled with cheese and smothered by a thick blonde cheese sauce the consistency of bisque.

Portion sizes in Europe are Liliputian compared to those in America, but this restaurant charitably proffered servings on plates the size of hub caps. I ate my plateful—though I probably shouldn't have—though Gopal could barely make a dent in his family-sized vegetarian pizza for one.

Excessively sated, I waddled back to the office, where we worked off and on until closing time.

At the end of the day, our Brussels host—a cheerful, kewpie doll-looking waif named Ann-led Gopal, Ann and me around the corner to a neighborhood tavern for a cocktail. We accessed the bar through a door so narrow and practically invisible that if not led by a native I would've completely missed it.

A leather-skinned female bartender with spiked blonde hair, think Tina Turner's 80s look, welcomed us with a friendly, "Bon soir" (sounds like "bone swah," and is French for "Good evening"). Gopal and kewpie-doll Ann—both non-drinkers—ordered soda, while manager-Ann and I ordered Maes drafts. I espied hanging on a nearby wall a poster of Elvis Presley in the later years—fifty pounds overweight, white jumpsuit, a pink lei hung around his neck—and I immediately felt a kinship with the owners, and a longing for home.

For dinner that evening, the desk clerk at our hotel recommended an area of town just a short walk away which, in his words, abounded with dining options. But after a *long* walk we found an overabundance of nothing, a few options offering nothing suitable for our collective appetites. So we double-backed to the Grahnd Ploss, where a block away we happened upon a restaurant named "La Maison de Crépes'.

The House of Crépes.

They asked my opinion, and I mentioned that I'd never eaten crépes before.

"What is it?" I asked.

"It's like a stuffed pancake," Ann said.

"Isn't it a dessert?"

"It is, but you can get it stuffed with anything, like ham or vegetables."

"Oh, you'll like it," they ensured me after a pregnant pause, knowing my finicky tastes.

I decided to try something new for a change—you may remember it; around 9:00 p.m. Brussels time (2:00 p.m. Central time), the earth would've been shaking—though not without some trepidation.

We pulled together two sidewalk tables and ate crêpes for dinner. I actually enjoyed mine; it really was like a stuffed pancake, squarely folded and stuffed with ham, cheese and egg (jambón, fromáge and oeuf, in French). It was a cool evening—both literally and figuratively, sitting at a sidewalk café, eating a relaxed dinner in a scenic urban setting, pedestrians passing at our shoulders.

After dinner, the prospects of dessert beckoned again. The group deferred to me—the chocoholic—to select our destination and I chose Haagen-Dasz, where I knocked my cravings into submission with a triple chocolate concoction—chocolate ice cream with brownies and a ribbon of chocolate syrup. Gopal's experience, however, went mostly unsatisfied.

He really wanted an ice-cream-topped waffle but settled on a basic ice cream cone because the pimple-faced teenager behind the counter explained they were out of waffles (despite the many eye-catching samples in the window display). This grew more complicated in the following minutes when a waitress served a tray full of ice cream-topped waffles to a table of ladies behind us, effectively raising Gopal's dander to a level I hadn't seen before.

"I feel discriminated," he declared, smiling though clearly perturbed. He half-heartedly spooned ice cream from his waffle cone, ogling the other table's desserts over his shoulder. Ann caught his eye, and we all shared a healthy chuckle when he realized we'd been watching him.

We returned to the hotel and turned in for the night. I phoned Lana after midnight, dinnertime in Collierville. She recapped their day and how active they've been over the Labor Day weekend. I could hear the boys' lively voices in the background, playing outside, and I suddenly had the urge for a game of catch.

I turned off the light around 1:00 a.m. and soon fell asleep, my head filled with wistful visions of gleaming bleachers and manicured baseball diamonds, a father alternating baseball tosses from one son to the other, kicking up puffs of dust with sneakered feet, broad smiles on their faces, content in each other's presence, not a worry in the world.

By the next morning, jet lag faded into a distant memory. I slept firmly and completely, barely turning over in six hours of rest, hazy recollections of a car horn blaring below my fifth floor—but numbered '4' on the lift—window the only hint of an interruption to my slumber. I slithered out of bed a little after 7:00, donned my running gear, and descended the lift to meet Gopal for a morning jog.

Clearly visible from the lobby, I awaited on the sidewalk across the narrow street from the hotel, the six feet of sidewalk at the main entrance being hose-sprayed by a hotel employee. I stretched my legs, allowing my GPS tracker to connect to a satellite, which I suspected would be difficult given the tall buildings and cloudy skies.

Gopal arrived right on time and we warmed up by walking uphill from the hotel, the cobbled sidewalks mostly vacant save for a smattering of briefcase-toting workers rushing to and fro, past the cathedral and the local office that would be our business home during our time in Brussels, to the top of Treurenberg Hill, which leveled out at a main artery crowded with sluggish traffic and bordering our destination: a park fronting the Royal Palace of Brussels, or Palais Royal de Bruxelles.

Situated in the Royal Quarter, the Palais Royal, or King's Palace, was a blend of different buildings assembled over time. The original building—the Couldenberg Palace—was destroyed by fire in 1731 and replaced by the current structure, the official home of the Belgian royal family, but they don't live there anymore. Now it contained the king's offices and was used only for state functions.

The King's Palace overlooked the Parc de Bruxelles (Brussels Park), our desired running spot, which dated to 1820. It was rectangular and roughly a mile around (I could've pinpointed the exact distance if not for my GPS tracker freezing up. I must've confused the poor thing, trying to use it 4,500 miles from home). Unpaved paths traced the park's perimeter, with additional paths—paved and unpaved—that crossed both vertically, horizontally, and diagonally. I read later that the middle axis of the park marked both the middle peristyle—a columned porch in Roman architecture—of the palace and the middle of the Belgian Federal Parliament building, which faced the other side of the park. The two facing buildings reportedly symbolized Belgium's system of government: a constitutional monarchy.

The King of Belgium was just a ceremonial leader (Belgium is a democracy, making him a constitutional monarch, similar to Queen Elizabeth), rubber stamping legislative and judicial actions. The Belgian constitution stipulated the king could take no official action without the approval of a minister, and his ministers were held accountable for the king's actions.

Gopal was relatively new to the sport of running, so we agreed to jog leisurely, with him dictating the pace. After one and a half laps, Gopal desired a rest, so I logged another lap at a faster pace and found him where we separated. I had tucked a camera in my fanny pack and we snapped photos each other in front of the King's Palace.

We walked downhill to the hotel, where I showered, dropped off some laundry, changed our hotel reservations (we planned to depart a day early for Paris), and readied ourselves for breakfast.

We weren't due in the office until 10:00, so we ate at a comfortable pace before strolling to the office mid-morning. Tuesday's agenda was lighter than the day before, so we busied ourselves during the remaining hours with email, coordinating our travel plans for the next week, and other work.

We suggested to Ann the Local that perhaps a more low-key lunch was in order, so she led us on a stroll to a nearby Metro subway station where she often ordered take-out sandwiches. Gopal and I broke away from the two Anns soon thereafter as we needed cash first.

"We'll only be a few minutes," I said.

Famous last words.

We walked two blocks uphill towards an ABN Amro Bank we'd spotted earlier. We'd been told that ABN Amro ATMs didn't charge Bank of America customers those annoying ATM fees when used by non-bank customers. We walked around the perimeter of the building but found no ATM.

So we turned back and walked downhill two blocks back to the Metro station, descending underground in search of an ATM that must be inside somewhere.

Nope.

We then ascended a long, steep staircase to street level and walked two blocks across a busy intersection teeming with lunch time traffic. Gopal had spotted an ING Bank nearby. We went inside and learned that its ATMs are for bank customers only.

But, fortunately, across the street stood a Fortis Bank, so we retraced our steps and waited in line at its ATM behind a woman who seemed to take excessive time with her withdrawal. She turned around and extended her palms skyward, shrugged her shoulders, saying something to me in French, or Dutch, I don't know. So I stepped forward and inserted my ATM card.

Nothing happened.

It wasn't working.

<Sigh>

"Now where do we go?" I huffed, thrusting my wallet in a rear pocket.

Gopal walked to the street and surveyed the landscape.

"Let's go that way," he said after a pause, pointing past the busy intersection, downhill two more blocks, where a steady stream of pedestrians filled the sidewalk, suddenly appearing and disappearing behind tall buildings at either corner.

So we walked.

As we approached the bottom of the hill, Gopal extended an upturned palm back over his shoulder, gesturing with his other hand toward a Citibank office a short distance away.

I slapped his palm, high-five style.

After withdrawing some euros, we hiked back to the train station, bought sandwiches, and toted them to the office, where the ladies awaited, having already finished theirs, curious to our delay, then amused by our adventure ("Such guys," they probably thought.)

Our afternoon consisted of administrative work, and we ended the day with another evening of savory Belgian cuisine.

Before dining, Gopal and Ann wanted to see St. Michael's Cathedral, so we dropped our briefcases at the hotel and grabbed our cameras, snapping as many photos as possible in the ten minutes before the doors closed. We ate dinner under a covered court off the Rue d'Arenberg, the restaurant tucked inside a gray marble-floored plaza, with welcoming sidewalk tables and a diverse menu with plentiful options suiting each of our tastes.

We followed dinner with another dessert quest, joking that we must follow our tradition—our three-day tradition—to pursue dessert after dinner, but at a different venue than the night before. Ann desired a waffle because she would return to America from our next stop in Paris and, unlike us, would have no more opportunities to enjoy another Belgian waffle dessert.

We decided on a brasserie across the Grahnd Ploss from where we ate our first waffle dessert two nights earlier. Each of us ordered a waffle midoku style, which is a Belgian waffle sprinkled with powdered sugar, topped by chocolate sauce and a scoop of vanilla ice cream.

Delicioso!!

During dessert, we struck up a conversation with a friendly middle-aged couple from Victoria, Canada, who admired our desserts. We learned their travels had followed ours in reverse (they had stopped in Brussels after three days in Paris with plans to visit Amsterdam next), but I was particularly interested in getting clarification on an earlier question they'd asked our French-speaking waiter about light shows in the plaza. They said that two light shows would be held in the Grahnd Ploss that evening, at 10:30 and 11:00 p.m., one hour hence.

Speaking of our waiter, he had an annoying, if not patronizing, practice of gazing over our heads while speaking to us, this while standing barely a foot away. We jokingly discussed in his absence what traumatic events from his past were at the root of his strange behavior.

We paid the bill and hurried to our hotel to pack unneeded clothes and miscellaneous items in a FedEx box, which we would ship home to alleviate the weight of our bulging suitcases, and to make our travels easier in the following week when we spent no more than two days in any city.

We returned to the Grahnd Ploss at precisely 10:30, where a large crowd craned their necks in the darkened square, flickering lights highlighting the striking architecture of the Town Hall, its more impressive features backlit in vibrant colors. Theatrical music, mostly classical, echoed through the square, setting the mood. The show lasted fifteen minutes and concluded with rousing applause.

The following evening, the three of us would catch a high-speed train to Paris, where we'd stay until the weekend. After that, our daily travels would take us to Germany, the Netherlands and back to Brussels.

Which reminded me of the old adage, accurate as ever: "No rest for the weary."

The author posing in front of the Royal Palace of Brussels, the official home of the Belgian royal family.

Stroking the Everard t'Serclaes monument in Brussels's Grand Place will reportedly bring good luck.

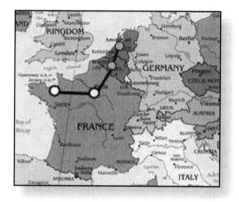

CHAPTER 3

Vive la France!

My maternal grandparents followed my travels from their long-time home of Bells, Tennessee; a tiny hamlet 15 minutes northwest of my hometown of Jackson, Tennessee. There was no more computer-savvy senior than my grandmother, 83 at the time. She printed my emailed travel blog for the benefit of my then-86-year-old grandfather, who wasn't computer-literate, but the volume of paper required to print my daily missives prompted her to teach him how to use a mouse to scroll through my email journals.

My European travels, by far the most extensive in my life, paled by comparison to their worldwide journeys.

I remember a framed world map mounted above a couch in their living room. Dozens and dozens of colored push pins pressed into the map denoted the countries both they and their children—my mother and two aunts—had visited. It was impressive—then and especially now—to reflect on the quantity of their travels, which included, most memorably, African safaris and European travels using my great-grandfather's World War I journal as a guide. There wasn't a continent they hadn't visited, except for Antarctica. My grandfather's aversion to the cold is so renowned in my family that we've ignored his eccentricities, like wearing wool socks in the stifling summer heat.

I should be so fortunate to have experiences such as theirs, not to mention a long and healthy life, a close-knit extended family, and, perhaps most impressively, over sixty-six years of marriage until my grandfather's death in 2008.

Our final day in Brussels began in a most unhurried manner. Gopal awoke early to use the hotel's Finnish sauna but Ann and I declined. Having stayed up past 1:00 a.m. each of the previous two nights, I looked forward to sleeping in, which I did, awaking around 9:00 a.m., pleasantly surprised to see rays of sunlight peeking through the gap in the drapes.

I threw on a T-shirt and shorts and went down for breakfast. Ann and Gopal had both dressed for work and packed their belongings. They graciously waited for me as I showered and packed, and we checked out together, leaving our suitcases in the hotel's locked luggage room, before strolling in the morning sunshine to the local office.

One of the first things I did upon connecting my laptop to the network was to satisfy a curiosity from the previous night. As we strolled around the Grand Place evaluating restaurant menus for dessert options, we came across a curious monument underneath the arcades of a house to the left of the Town Hall. A crowd of people stood at the monument, running their hands over it lovingly, almost reverentially.

The monument portrayed the figure of a shrouded man lying nearly prone on the ground, its striking gold features contrasting with centuries of grime covering the rest of the building. The date '1388' had been carved into the stone, but the lack of English descriptions left us wondering about the monument's meaning.

We followed the crowd's lead, stepping forward and running our hands over the monument, foot to head, touching also the face of a tiny cherub, a dog, and a shield. As we walked away, we speculated about its meaning. I guessed that it portrayed Christ after the Crucifixion and, no better idea proffered, everyone agreed that it seemed a logical conclusion.

I wasn't even close.

The monument underneath the arcades of the Maison de l'Étoile house at the Brussels Grand Place commemorates Everard t'Serclaes, a popular 14th-century Brussels hero. To make a long story short, t'Serclaes was caught up in a territorial feud with the Lord of Gaasbeek, who had his castle just outside Brussels. In 1388, when riding alone on the road from Brussels to a nearby town, Serclaes was ambushed by Gaasbeek's bailiff and bastard son, who chopped off one of his feet and cut his tongue. The Brussels hero was transported to the Maison de l'Étoile, where he died. The Brussels citizens avenged Serclaes' death by storming and destroying the Gaasbeek castle, pillaging its chicken pens and feasting on the chickens (a historical precursor to the movement promoting free-range fowls). This event has earned the Brusselers the nickname of "kiekenfretters", i.e. "chicken-eaters".

Anyway, local superstition dictated that stroking the statue, especially Serclaes' arm and the dog's nose, brought good luck.

I'm not sure I felt any luckier than yesterday, but my curiosity had been satisfied.

A few hours of email checking and meeting preparations quickly passed; before we knew it, the lunch hour had snuck upon us. Gopal departed first, joining an Indian colleague for lunch at an Indian restaurant (in their conversations, they learned that their families lived a very short distance from each other in Chennai). Ann and I, however, worked another thirty minutes before venturing to a Greek café I'd spotted during my walking jaunt the day we arrived. I had a serious hankering for a gyro and Ann, whose grandparents are first generation Greek immigrants, agreed almost immediately.

The restaurant—called Pita Greek Creta—faced a triangular cobbled square—the plaza d'Espagne—about a block from the Grahnd Ploss. Large trees shaded much of the square, and dozens of pigeons lounged atop a sculpture of a seated man on the rim of a scenic fountain. Baby blue cloudless skies allowed the brilliant sunshine to warm the air, which brought out a sizeable crowd seated at sidewalk tables sheltered by multi-colored umbrellas.

I ordered a pita gyro (layers of shaved lamb, lettuce and white tzatziki sauce in a swollen pocket of pita bread) and Ann shared with me some of her faláfel (a mixture of chick peas, garbanzo beans and spices and pressed into small thick medallions). I hadn't eaten a decent gyro since my mid-nineties stint with Delta Air Lines, when I often drove a short distance from company headquarters to a hole-in-the-wall Greek café within sight of Atlanta Hartsfield Airport. The Brussels gyro tasted wonderfully, but those in Atlanta remained the best I'd ever eaten.

Following lunch, I escorted Ann to a nearby ATM so she could withdraw some euros. We started back to the office when I asked—in a teasing tone but with sincerity—whether she wanted dessert.

"I can go for some ice cream," she said, so we set out to find a suitable parlor.

We stopped at a nearby ice cream stand when Ann turned around and gazed at something behind me.

"Isn't that the plaza?" she asked, referring to the covered plaza on the Rue d'Arenberg where we ate dinner the previous night.

I knew right away what she was thinking.

"Newhaus?" I asked, smiling.

She nodded, and we made a beeline for the Newhaus chocolate store.

To preclude any doubt in your collective minds, the chocolate in Europe is, without question, the absolute best in the world! I love American chocolate (Ghirardelli and Hershey's, to wit) but the exceptional quality and fine taste of European chocolate—particularly the Belgian and Swiss varieties—makes comparing European and American chocolates similar to comparing, say, Harrods and Wal-mart. Simply put, there is no comparison.

Chocolateurs abounded at every corner, it seemed; some brands I recognized (e.g., Godiva, Toblerone, Cadbury) but many others I didn't, including Newhaus, which Ann said was better than Godiva, which was arguably the best premium chocolate in the world.

An ice cream stand outside the store offered a dozen flavors, but one stood out: 'chocolat noir', deep brunette and oh so tempting. I could hear it calling my name. Ann did, too; her name, that is.

A sign instructed us in four languages to pay at the register inside before receiving our ice cream. Once inside, a fragrant aroma of chocolate enveloped us, rendering me speechless. Breathing air so deliciously chocolatey, I joked with the proprietor whether he would allow me to work there for the balance of the day.

Newhaus is a Belgian brand, founded in 1857 by a Swiss confectioner named Jean Newhaus living in Brussels. It billed itself as "the absolute market leader in the luxury praline sector in Belgium and Luxembourg since 1991" with annual sales in the $75-100 million range.

This particular store presented its wares in plain view, not boxed like in many chocolate shops, instead individually stacking and aligning its products like little chocolate families. We wandered around the small store, savoring the sights and smells. Temptations urged me to open my wallet and spend freely, but I found some willpower for once, buying only a double scoop of ice cream and one milk chocolate bar.

We exited through the front door and an Asian man scooped our orders, placing each in a medium-sized tapered sugar cone wrapped in a white napkin. Ann received hers first. By the time I received mine, I heard her grunting behind me. Turning around, Ann's eyes rolled upward, as though praising God for the delectable treat in her hand.

"Dish ith su gd," she mumbled.

One bite elevated me to similar state of chocolatey bliss.

"Mmm hmm," I muttered, my mouth full of ice cream. "Dish ITH su gd."

Actually, it was BETTER than 'so good'. It was sinful!

I found Newhaus ice cream to be richer than that in America. It melted almost immediately, not from the heat but its consistency, lighter, almost gelatinous, with a watery sheen. We stood rooted in one spot and ate most of it, not wanting it to drip on our clothes, which invariably happens to me when I attempt to simultaneously walk and eat. For the next hour, we couldn't stop gushing about how wonderful it tasted, and Ann best described it as "divine."

"This is how God intended ice cream to taste," I declared after I finished, tossing my napkin in a street-corner trash bin. Ann agreed.

The anticipation of riding a high-speed train was almost too exciting to bear. I'd ridden many subways but never a true "passenger" train.

It was a long walk to the Brussels Central Station, across cobbled sidewalks with packed suitcases, our train's platform a long march through a maze of underground tunnels, up and down stairs, the directional signs in French and Flemish. Fortunately, Ann the Local accompanied us to Paris, and she expertly led us to our platform.

We had reservations for the Thalys train, locally called the TGV (a French acronym for *train à grande vitesse*, or high-speed train), a pan-European rail linking Paris, Brussels, Amsterdam and Cologne.

Each Thalys train included eight non-smoking cars, or carriages, with two classes of service: first (called Comfort 1) and second (Comfort 2). Three of the eight carriages were dedicated to Comfort 1, four for Comfort 2, the eighth being a bar carriage. Total seating could accommodate 350-400 people.

The trains crossed the roughly 175 miles between Brussels and Paris in just shy of 90 minutes, with peak speeds reaching 300 km/h (a NASCAR-ish 185 mph).

We boarded a Comfort 1 carriage and found our assigned seats in a facing 2x2 row, a table separating us. Ann the Local and I had spacious 'venster', or window, seats; Ann the Manager and Gopal sat next to the 'gang', or aisle.

Train travel in Europe is affordable and pleasant, especially compared to air travel. Our Comfort 1 tariff was, at the time, only 98.50€, or about $120 (the current exchange rate hadn't been favorable for American dollars; $1 worth roughly 75€ cents). Trains are an oft-used means of European transportation; in the cities, within countries, and certainly across borders. Europe is so compact with short distances between major cities that it often makes more sense to travel by train than plane.

Our train pulled away from the platform at its prescribed time (7:40 p.m.). Our attendant—a tall, lean Scandinavian lady dressed in a ruby red uniform and cap, her long blonde hair pulled back in a ponytail—soon appeared and offered us moist towelettes, which Gopal gushed over, for they were sizeable and never seemed to lose its dampness.

"Now, *this* is a moist towelette," he gushed, wiping his hands and face twice-over. Then, gesturing to a pocket-sized pad I kept in my back pocket to take notes, he added, "You must put this in your writings."

And so I did.

Soon thereafter, a train official appeared at our row, requesting in French our tickets. We handed them over, at which point he inspected each closely and punched a pin-sized hole before returning each to us with a friendly, "Merci." The attendant followed shortly behind, reappearing with a serving cart.

"Vould you like to have lunch?" she asked, perkily.

Oui, I vould, I thought, choosing not to comment on her misstatement that lunch is served at noon not evening.

A full moon rose above the horizon as we consumed our meal: sliced ham and turkey with sides of tiny potato cubes, vegetable strips and bread. Offered the choice of water, soda or beer, I chose the latter, a Belgian beer called Stella Artois, known informally as a "pincher", which Ann the Local explained is a 'beginner' or 'starter' beer, weaker than the more robust and filling beers and lagers (Maes beer is also a 'pincher'). One might drink it for happy hour or after sporting activities before progressing to a more premium beer, like drinking PBR before Sam Adams.

Pleasant conversation passed the time during our meal, bucolic Belgian and French landscapes framed outside our window (if we were really going 300 km/h, it sure didn't feel like it). The panoramic vistas weren't unlike what you find in the rural Southern U.S.: rolling fields dominated by the color green, occasionally broken by sections of tilled brown earth awaiting the next crop, farm machinery crawling down winding roads, cattle grazing in fields, gothic church spires peeking above the rooftops of small villages.

Perhaps the biggest difference were the houses, none constructed with wood frame or stucco, virtually all were brick, some stone, with red slate roofs and set close together like people on a crowded bus. A scenic panorama, yes, but not quite the "Wow!" settings I had envisioned.

Our conversation digressed into a humorous discussion about the differences between train and plane travel. The more we talked, the harder we laughed, and my seatmates openly encouraged me to take notes.

The hilarity resulted in the following Top 10 Differences between Train and Plane Travel, David Lettterman-style:

10. Seat belts not required.
9. Tray tables can be kept in their downright and unlocked positions.
8. Moist towelettes that double as body cleansers.
7. Perky Scandinavian train attendants.
6. Security lines? Baggage check? What are those?
5. Bright overhead lights that illuminate the worst of your complexion (and can't be turned off).
4. No waiting until cruising altitude to power on your electrical equipment.

3. Allowed to carry on the biggest honking bottle of water you can hold.

2. Able to retrieve your baggage before the train comes to a complete stop.

And the number one difference between train and plane travel?

1. Food. REAL food.

Ta da!

The clock struck nine when we screeched to a halt at the Paris Nord train station, a massive hangar of iron and steel, large timetables looming over the concourse, its fast-flipping letters and numbers going 'clickety-clack', just like in the movies. A taxi awaited us—prearranged on the train; one benefit of traveling Comfort 1—and our driver led us from the station and across a busy street to his parallel parked minivan (Taxis here are often nice cars. It's not uncommon to ride in a Mercedes or Audi; though I didn't take notice of ours, probably neither given it was a minivan).

I took a seat between Ann the Manager and Gopal, unbelieving that I actually sat on French soil, though the sentiment quickly wore off, as our taxi took us through typical urban settings, streets lined with closed shops protected by graffiti-covered metal shades, garbage strewn in the gutters, though the sight of wrought-iron balcony rails like those in the New Orleans French Quarter uplifted me a bit.

A long ride led us to our hotel near Charles de Gaulle Airport on the outskirts of the city, an uninspiring area, high rise hotels the only landmarks of note, the famous sights of Paris miles away. I hoped to see more the next day, when we met our French colleagues at a FedEx station somewhere in the city. If not tomorrow—a Thursday, then perhaps Friday, or definitely Saturday, when I had the day to myself to roam, freely going wherever impulse directed me.

Though excited to be in Paris, my first impressions were mediocre, at best, but perhaps I shouldn't have been so hard on the city. Most airports have the attractiveness and charm of a three-toed sloth, so I gave Paris some slack.

But it would've been nice if there was at least one English-speaking channel other than CNN, whose reception was spotty and sound almost unintelligible without cranking up the volume. Watching dubbed reruns of 'Xena: Warrior Princess' did nothing for me.

"Voolait, Xena! Voolait!"

Bonne journée mes amis et famille (Good day, my friends and family)

Je suis à Paris (I am in Paris)

Votre mère est un hamster et vos odeurs de père des wildeberries (Your mother is a hamster and your father smells of wildeberries.)

I couldn't resist a little Monty Python humor while testing my new favorite Internet site: Language translators. I needed it to interpret an email from my grandmother that was totally in French.

Five minutes on the translator and I had it decoded.

Anyhow, I awoke my first day in Paris a little lethargic. The air conditioner in my room blew only hot air, so I tossed and turned all night, the heavier spreads discarded to the floor, leaving only the bed sheet, which couldn't prevent the sweaty mess I became come sunrise.

With no Internet access in my room, I moseyed down to the business center early to check email, followed by an early morning treadmill workout in the salon (what they called the fitness center).

We converged in the lobby for a spartan breakfast, after which we hailed a cab to ferry us to one of the metropolitan FedEx stations.

This particular FedEx station was located in an industrial area north of the city center—where the famous tourist sites are—but inside the expressway ring, a roughly 20-square mile loop packed with the majority of Paris' million-plus population. Sheet metal warehouses and tall smoldering smokestacks dominated the scenery, and I lamented quietly that I hadn't yet seen any of the *real*—read, touristy—Paris.

Once we found the entrance to the building, we introduced ourselves to the receptionist and asked for our host. Soon thereafter, footfalls on the concrete steps echoed in the stairwell over our heads. A handsome young Frenchman then appeared, a broad smile spanning his face. He looked debonair in a short-sleeved red striped shirt and blue tie, a full head of hair moussed and slicked back. He introduced himself as Pascal and led us upstairs to a large conference room where our meeting would take place.

We met for two hours, followed by lunch at a sandwich shop across the street. I ordered my sandwich in French—with a little coaching by Pascal, successfully completing the transaction without a word of English (though not without a lot of hand gestures and finger pointing).

It struck me that I'd spoken more French in the past three days than in my entire life, despite my severely limited vocabulary: yes (oui), no (no), please (si vu plait), thank you (mercî), good day (bon jour), good evening (bon soir), goodbye (au revoir). For obvious reasons, my French fell out of the mouth rather than rolled off the tongue, and whenever I spoke I was bothered by a feeling of awkwardness, like a child learning a new skill and looking to his parents for reinforcement.

I understood that many Parisians spoke English but refused, although if you were friendly and showed good manners—politely asking if they spoke English (Parlez-vous anglais?), then they would more likely offer an English response.

Our afternoon included the company of a FedEx account executive—named Christophe—who led us on a sales call to a FedEx customer and importer of film and television electronics. The customer was a delightful lady—an engaging middle-aged woman with large glasses framed by unkempt blonde shoulder-length hair—who eagerly answered our every question and seemed genuinely pleased when we presented her with a FedEx gift upon our departure.

Ann the Local—who joined us on the call, her first sales call—had decided to return to Brussels a day early, so Christophe deposited her at a train station, then drove out of his way to play tour guide for Gopal and me, detouring to the Paris city center, showing us major sites up close and personal: the Eiffel Tower, the Arc de Triomphe, the Champs-Élysées, the Louvre museum, and many others.

Once back at the station, Ann the Manager sat alone at a table in front of her laptop—she had volunteered to stay behind because five people wouldn't fit in Christophe's compact car. We checked email for an hour; Gopal catching a seated cat nap, his head balanced precariously on his slumped shoulders. We left around seven, in search of a cab to take us into the city for dinner.

I asked the ladies at the front desk for advice where to best hail a cab, but they spoke no English, so we set out on our own, walking in what we thought was the best direction.

Twenty minutes later, we found ourselves deep—and I'm talking Mariana Trench deep—in the heart of an industrial center, not a single cab in sight, traffic dwindling with every block. The sun hung low in the sky and we knew the time had come to ask for help.

We chose a small Chinese business—Samly, by the name painted on a truck parked out front. It was full of activity, dark-skinned men busily loaded pallets of rice paper and foodstuffs on a truck emblazoned with a curious-looking logo that resembled a hairless red beaver. Gopal and Ann went inside to seek help. I hung out on the sidewalk in the event a cab ventured by.

I waited ten minutes before they reemerged from the office. I caught Gopal's eye across the road, inquiring with a hopeful 'thumbs up' as to their success. He responded, thumbs down, frowning, and I wondered, "What in the world are we going to do?"

"They don't speak English," he lamented, and Ann added, "He was lying."

Those are cold people, I thought, assuming that meant the businesspeople knew English but refused to speak it, spiting our nationality. Then Gopal burst out a deep belly laugh, and I then realized that Ann actually had said, "He *is* lying", meaning Gopal.

"The cab will be here in seven minutes," he said.

WHEW!

Crisis averted.

We stood on the street corner, the sky uniformly drowning into the darkness of night, Ann and Gopal entertaining me with the story how they won their cooperation.

Ann thought their chances would be better if she played the role of distressed English-speaking woman desperate for help. Gopal wasn't convinced but went along.

They pushed open the front door and Ann, in her best Meryl Streep impression, acted the part perfectly, her expression fraught with worry, rubbing fake tears from her eyes with a knuckle, pleading with the owner, her voice cracking, "Taxi . . . si . . . vu . . . plait?"

It worked.

"Oh, you need taxi?" responded a lady behind the counter, immediately picking up the phone.

Seven minutes later, we sat in a taxi headed for a 6th District Indian restaurant that Ann and Gopal had found on the Internet.

The 6th District was in the Left Bank area of the Paris city center. According to my AAA Europe TravelBook, most Parisians mentally divided their city into two halves—Left Bank and Right Bank—split by the meandering Seine River. Traditionally, the Right Bank stood for order and elegance, typified by the monumental architecture running from the Louvre to the Arc de Triomphe, while the Left Bank was an altogether more stylish place, the artistic and cultural center, where Ernest Hemingway and other famous authors of yore thrived during their heydays.

Our taxi deposited us in front of a quaint but first-rate Indian restaurant—Yugaraj—on the Rue Dauphine, a stone's throw from one of the city's uibiquitous Seine River bridges. We ate a tranquil dinner, each selecting different options from a set menu—the Star of India menu—which included a limited selection of appetizers, entrées and desserts, though my first inclination was to order the only entrée I recognized—tandoori chicken, which I'd previously eaten at a popular Indian restaurant in Memphis—but Gopal wouldn't let me, teasingly encouraging me to step "out of the box" and try something new.

This teasing was an ongoing effort by Gopal to 'loosen me up' (his words, not mine). He thought I asked too many questions about pending plans and activities, that I should just "go with the flow" and whatever happened, happened. We had different personalities—he leaned to the political left, I to the right; our ages being another barometer (he in his early 30s while I approached 40). Our diversity was rarely a sticking point, however, and we balanced each other well.

I took Gopal's advice and ordered from the Star of India menu: an appetizer of samosas, dinner of tandoori pork, and dessert of homemade ice cream flavored with almonds and pistachio nuts.

After I finished my appetizer (samosas are a racquetball-sized fried appetizer with a filling of assorted vegetables), Gopal, still needling my apprehensions, asked in his best telemarketing voice, "So, Mr. Martindale, on a scale of one to ten, how would you describe your dining experience thus far?"

Playing along, I answered, "Well, the samosas were indeed delicious. I would give it an 8.5."

"Is there anything we could have done to make that a nine or nine point five?"

I stroked my chin, pensively considering the question.

"You could've covered it in chocolate sauce," I replied, and the table broke out into hearty laughter.

Dinner concluded around ten and we emerged from the restaurant, the sidewalks bustling with diners, tourists and locals, headed in the direction of the Seine, in search of a riverfront brasserie for dessert.

Crossing the bridge, something alit caught my peripheral vision and I turned my head, announcing to my comrades, "Hey! Check it out!"

Glittering lights on the Eiffel Tower gleamed like Christmas tassel or, as Ann described it, millions of sparkling diamonds, about two-thirds of the tower viewable above the treetops lining the Seine, an intense spotlight rotating counter-clockwise at its crown. Perhaps there was music accompanying the light show, inaudible to us given the considerable distance. We stood, impressed, expecting a variety of shimmering lights. However, the scene remained unchanged. So the interest wore thin after a few minutes and we continued across the bridge, our destination a brasserie a few blocks away, Gopal making corny puns as we walked ("What language do they speak in France? Seine language.")

Gopal and I, still dressed in suits, our collars loosened, tied tucked safely in our jacket pockets, claimed adjacent sidewalk tables at the Café du Pont-Neuf on the northern bank, or quai, of the Seine. We plopped into adjacent chairs and dropped our briefcases with a thud on the sidewalk. Ann and Gopal ordered espressos; I hot chocolate and a chocolate crepe. Cars and taxis moved stealthily on the busy street, and we commented, tongue-in-cheek, that we'd have little trouble hailing a taxi for the ride to our hotel.

The midnight hour rapidly approaching and tired from the long day, we quickly consumed our desserts, eager to return to the hotel. We summoned a cab almost instantly, and crammed ourselves in the rear seat, an interminable thirty minute ride being sandwiched in the middle, my tight hamstrings begging for mercy.

We arrived about 11:30 p.m., though it would've been earlier had we possessed the hotel address to present our driver, who knew the area but not the hotel's location. Once in my room, I tossed my suit atop the neighboring twin, plopped down on the other, and heaved a sigh before phoning home.

I set my trusted travel clock for 6:15 the following morning and quickly drifted off to sleep, aided by cooling drafts wafting in through an open window.

Morning arrived early but almost too late.

My travel alarm failed to go off at the prescribed hour, so it was by luck that I squinted at the TV clock and read the time: 7:01 a.m., one minute past the hour we agreed to meet for breakfast.

I leapt out of bed and hurriedly readied myself (that's one benefit of being a guy: brush your teeth and wipe a wet wash rag under your arms and you're ready to go). I found Ann seated in the hotel restaurant ten minutes later, Gopal nowhere in sight. He arrived ten minutes after that, wearing a golf shirt, shorts and sandals, miffed that housekeeping had not brought him the iron and ironing board he had prearranged the night before.

We gobbled up breakfast—I awoke too abruptly to have an appetite, so I ate only two croissants. Gopal returned to his room to change while I arranged for a taxi to take us to the Paris Montparnasse train station.

A lady at the front desk suggested we allow an hour and a half transit time to the station, though it became crystal clear halfway into our taxi ride that the volume of cars clogging the expressway would threaten our departure.

Gopal asked the driver—a friendly Chinese man who knew enough English to be dangerous—how far to the station.

"Forty minute," he answered.

I looked at my watch, then at Gopal, shaking my head.

Our train would depart in forty minutes.

We needed to find another way.

Gopal explained we had a 9:05 a.m. train to catch. The driver consulted his city plan—a detailed city map for taxi drivers—and advised he would find another route, though we would have little time to locate our train when we arrived.

The subsequent minutes transpired like an amusement park ride: sudden accelerations and stops, hairpin turns negotiated at high speeds pressing me against the door, not that any of his maneuvers struck other drivers as aggressive or unexpected. French drivers aren't what I would call "considerate". They are assertive but not aggressive, every driver for himself, offering little latitude to other commuters, finding every soft spot in traffic as a means to advance further, like a flowing river circling a stone, finding the most direct path with the least resistance.

The tension in my face must have been palpable but I tried to suppress it.

Twenty minutes to go and we were many miles away.

Then fifteen.

Ten.

Still not there.

"I get you there," assured the driver. "You have five minute to find train."

And he was exactly right.

We threw open the taxi doors at 9:00 a.m., with five minutes to negotiate an unfamiliar train station. Darting inside, we quickly located the timetable: our train waited on platform five.

Four minutes to go.

We dashed two steps at a time down the escalator.

Three minutes to go.

We ran down platform five.

Two minutes to go.

The train departed.

But, fortunately, not without us on board.

Two minutes after we sat down in our Comfort 1 seats, the train pulled away from the platform, right on time.

I spent the two hours in transit to Rennes (sounds like 'wren') writing in my journal, admiring the pastoral scenes framed in the window, similar to those I witnessed on our journey from Brussels, one major difference being dozens of windmills—resembling slowly-spinning Mercedes logos atop hundred foot tapered towers—that supplied power to rural areas.

After our arrival in Rennes, I called our local contact on my cell phone as I couldn't get the pay phone to accept my credit card (I cringed when thinking of the roaming charges!). He was somewhere in the station, awaiting our arrival. Soon after, I saw him descending the staircase, talking into a cord dangling from his earpiece.

His name was Jean-Francois, a bookish, wiry man with stylish wire-rimmed glasses, dapperly dressed in a grey pinstripe suit, thinning hair that belied his youthful features. We shook hands and he asked us to call him 'Jeff'—"Iz easier for za American to speak," he said (I don't think we called him by his informal name even once.)

Jean-Francois took us on a mini-tour of Rennes, pointing out interesting points of note for our project, driving us around in his compact Ford Focus, its leather seats still preserving a new car smell.

A GPS navigator embedded in the dash presented in two-dimensional detail every feature of the road system (most taxis have them, too).

We headed away from town for a 70 km ride to a coastal town called Saint-Malo (sounds like 'san ma-LOW'). Jean Francois' sales territory was the Brittany region of northwest France, a scenic peninsula bordered on the north by the English Channel, the west by the Atlantic Ocean, and the south by the Bay of Biscay.

A popular tourist attraction, the walled city of Saint-Malo was a small charming city, lively and full of character. Originally in the Middle Ages, Saint-Malo was a fortified island situated at the mouth of the Rance. It was destroyed by the Germans during World War II then rebuilt afterwards exactly the way it was before. It was the most visited place in Brittany and served as a key port linking Brittany with England via the English Channel.

Our local meeting wouldn't begin for several hours, so Jean-Francois treated us to lunch at an enchanting restaurant atop the citadel on the coast of the English Channel—La Brasserie du Sillon. The maitre'd seated us at a corner table covered by fine linen. Immediately outside our window, a vast expanse of beach the color of khaki stretched in either direction. The tide drew the channel far out from the coast (at least three hundred yards, by my guess), and locals with buckets and special hooks probed the damp sand around exposed boulders for shrimp, crabs, and small rock lobsters.

Jean-Francois skillfully advised us on the items presented on the menu, written completely in French. We ordered from a set menu—appetizer, entrée and dessert (set menus are a common and affordable dining option). While my appetizer and entrée (sea bass) were quite tasty, my dessert was unlike anything I'd had before.

Chocolate soup.

I don't remember the French term for it, but my dessert was thicker than broth but thinner than Hershey's syrup and served in a bowl, whipped cream in the center, a warm chocolate cookie resting on the rim.

Mmm mmm good!

Lunch lasted almost two hours, which is consistent with most European dining experiences. In America, you can't go five minutes without a pimple-faced waitress—server, whatever—asking whether you needed something, delivering the check before you've even placed your fork on the plate following the final bite, eager to turn over the table, thereby generating more revenue.

In Europe, you can linger at your table as long as you please; it's part of the culture (now I understood the waiter's surprise at my fleeting hotel dining experience in Amsterdam). The server was never out of sight, they're content to wait in the shadows, approaching only occasionally, never pressing patrons to accelerate their pace. In fact, they won't bring you the check unless you specifically ask for it (which took a little getting used to). The slower, more relaxed pace had grown on me, and I expected it would be hard to re-assimilate into Western dining practices.

We were fifteen minutes late for our meeting, but Jean-Francois said not to worry, the customer wouldn't mind (another cultural difference between here and the States; in the U.S.; fifteen minutes late would earn you a stern rebuke if not an outright cold shoulder). The meeting went well, and our return drive to Rennes was filled with pleasant chatter and work talk.

As we neared Rennes, I reflected on the day. I liked Saint-Malo, though it was probably a more accurate statement to say that I liked the outlying, rural areas of France to the metropolitan area of Paris. Being a small-town boy, perhaps I identified with the pastoral settings and more relaxed lifestyle than the hustle and bustle of big city life (not that Rennes was a bucolic town. I was very surprised to learn later that Rennes had a half million residents).

We almost missed our return train as Rennes's city traffic stalled us about two blocks from the station with five minutes remaining before departure. I hated to interrupt Jean-Francois as he told us about his grandparents living in the Normandy region of France (where the Allies landed on D-Day in 1944), but we had a train to catch. So I cut his narrative short, hopped out of his Ford and we hoofed two blocks double time.

We boarded our train with two minutes to spare; the doors closing before we found our seats. I hate being late for anything, so to say that the day's travel adventures had caused me stress would be a gross understatement.

Upon reaching Paris after a two-hour train ride, we exited the train station in an unfamiliar part of the city and it took about an hour to get our bearings, find a subway station, find a second subway station when lines at the first were too long for our liking, and finally a third subway station when the automated ticket machine at the second wouldn't work. Once we boarded the subway—aka, the Metro—only twenty minutes separated us from the Pont Neuf, where Ann awaited at the same brasserie where we ended the prior day with espressos and dessert.

We found her sitting at a sidewalk table as we approached, and, boy, was she glad to see us. Not long after we loosened our ties and sat down beside her, she related, somewhat distressingly, that a man had been hitting on her, which under normal circumstances would've been flattering given the romantic setting, but he was unnervingly persistent, not to mention he used what is perhaps the lamest pickup line I've ever heard ("Mademoiselle, you have the most beautiful teeth I've ever seen.") It got so bad that Ann—a divorcée—switched a ring from her right hand to her left ring finger to give the impression of matrimonial ties in the hopes of purging the amorous but annoying stranger.

She'd already scouted a restaurant for dinner, so with hunger pangs growling in our bellies, we left the brasserie and Ann led us on a five minute walk down the Quai de Louvre and ducked into a neighboring block to an eatery—le Zimmer—near the Châtelet Metro station. Decorated in baroque elegance, the maitre'd led us to a table in the middle of the restaurant, its fringed seats covered with velvety cushions. Black-and-white pictures of semi-nude women hung on the wall—the pictures taken in the restaurant, it appeared—and we knew then that we'd entered a *real* French café.

Gopal ordered his usual vegetarian fare, and Ann and I both ordered pan fried sole with an appetizer of French onion soup, which I ordered only because my grandmother had suggested it ("When in France . . ." as they say, right?). The food was delicious, but the luster of eating in restaurants twice daily for a week began to wear off.

Midnight arrived soon after Gopal and I returned to our hotel after an hour's ride on the Metro. The work week finally over, anxious to be a tourist before catching a train to Cologne the following night, I looked forward to saying 'au revoir' to the demands of business and 'bon jour' to the familiar sights of Paris.

Being a tourist in Paris required a good bit of planning because time was fleeting and there was scarcely enough of it to visit the major sites in a short period of time. One must be content with visiting "must see" highlights lest time get away from you faster than Republicans from a tax hike.

Gopal and I previously discussed sightseeing strategies on the express subway to the airport as we both had similarly limited hours to see Paris. He wanted to spend most of his time at the Louvre Museum; I desired to split my time between the Eiffel Tower, Arc de Triomphe, and Champs-Élysées, squeezing in time for some shopping.

Ambitious? Perhaps, but I thought I could cover it.

We resolved to set a personal 'cutoff time', a FedEx term we adapted to define the hour at which our sightseeing must end. I established mine at 2:00 p.m., meaning no matter where I was in the city, I would leave then in order to allow ample time to return to the airport, grab my bags, and double back to my train station.

The day marked the first since my arrival in Europe that Gopal and I would not spend together. Actually, we would be separated for several days as his itinerary would take him to Berlin and Hamburg, mine to Cologne and Dusseldorf, where we'd reunite four days hence.

I ran into Gopal in the hallway around 7:30 a.m., me on the way to my room with a plate of croissants I would eat while packing, he in the opposite direction, his suitcase in tow, towards checkout before heading into Paris.

He had about an hour's lead on me by the time I finished packing and readying myself. I caught a hotel shuttle to the airport, where I planned to use a Metro day pass for access to the subway, which would carry me throughout the city.

When I reached the train station, I found to my heart's content a long line at the ticket counter and silently counted my blessings for the wisdom to buy a ticket the previous evening.

I confidently strode up to the Metro turnstile, inserted my stamp-sized pass into the appropriate slot, and leaned into the waist-high crossbar, which immediately locked, my momentum doubling me over the metal rod, the pressure on my testicles far exceeding its pain threshold.

"Excusez-moi," I said apologetically to the person behind me, reinserting the ticket to the same result.

I stepped back with furrowed brow, visually searching for the information desk. I had a sneaking suspicion what the hold-up might be, yet I presented my ticket at the information counter, explaining my predicament. He confirmed what I suspected.

A one-day pass is good for a calendar day, not a twenty-four hour period from when the ticket is purchased.

The ticket had expired at midnight.

Well, it would've been nice to know that when I bought it. That's what I get for assuming.

Anyhow, turning around to face the ticket line, I immediately regretted being so smug upon my arrival. I faced at least a forty-five minute wait, maybe longer, jeopardizing my already compressed sightseeing schedule. Figuring time was more precious than money, I bit the bullet and hailed a taxi.

A bushy-haired, mustachioed cabbie drove me into the city, him being the only one available who would accept credit cards (I had only ten euros in my wallet and the fare would be three times that). Twenty minutes later, he dropped me off at the Galeries Lafayette, forty-five minutes before the doors opened.

The nearby brasseries hadn't yet opened and I'd planned to read a book in the interim, but I espied a striking church framing the gap between the buildings where the narrow avenue came to an end.

A quick four-block walk down shaded streets as yet untouched by the morning sun brought me to Trinity Square (Square de Trinite), its centerpiece an eye-catching cathedral, surrounded by a manila blockade restricting entrance due to construction.

There wasn't much to see besides the church, so I doubled back from whence I came, eager to delve into a travel book I'd brought, though, when I came to the shops, I surprisingly found the doors to be open (the cabbie told me it wouldn't open until 10:00, but he erred a half hour on the late side).

The Galeries Lafayette, founded in 1896, is an eight-story shop on the Right Bank, near the famous Opera House. Excellently located at the heart of a shopping quarter in the Paris city center, it was well known for its fashion and novelty.

Ann had suggested this site the night before as a better, more affordable shopping option than, say, the high-priced designer boutiques lining the popular tourist avenues. I'm all for the affordable, though I didn't want to scrimp too much on price and quality as I knew Lana was 4,000 miles away playing single parent for two weeks while her husband traipsed around Europe writing emails home about how much fun he's having.

"You better bring me back something nice," she warned, I mean, suggested before I left, and I knew that if I spent my free day in Paris visiting tourist sites leaving little time for shopping then I was more likely to make a hasty (read 'ill-advised') purchase and I'd return home to a wife whose memento of her husband's trip would be a T-shirt reading, "My husband went to Paris and all he bought me was a Eiffel Tower miniature".

Anyway, once inside, I surveyed the retail landscape, evaluating my options. The ground floor consisted primarily of cosmetics; when I say "primarily" I mean there was enough make-up to coat the field at the Superdome.

The second floor wasn't any better: women's designer clothing. I'm not the most fashionable bloke who ever lived; my idea of high fashion is a shirt with a pattern on it. I wouldn't know a fashion designer if she pinned me to the ground and farted on my head. Needless to say, my presence in the high fashion section was like the ACLU attending the Southern Baptist Convention.

I ascended the escalator to another floor and found more affordable fashions in my price range: the retail version of a 99 cent menu, but would relax my penny-pinching standards for this occasion. I strolled around, examining pallid mannequins for possible fashions and colorful styles that Lana might like, making note of sales (there weren't many), committing to memory designer names and store locations so I could retrace my steps, if necessary.

I shopped for an hour (which by 55 minutes exceeded my normal shopping tolerance), narrowing the list of possibilities, checking my timepiece (not a watch but a FedEx clock and compass combo clipped on my belt loop with a carabiner), temporarily losing myself in the toy section, silently lamenting the lack of substantial toy sections and massive Toys R Us stores when I was a kid. The best option in the good ole days were holiday retail catalogs, which my younger brother and I wore thin from constant use, cataloging so many toys on our Christmas lists that my mother forced us to revise them to indicate which ones we *really* wanted Santa to bring.

I finally made a purchase and left the store in search of the Paris Opera House, which I understood to be nearby. I found it quickly;

multi-story vertical banners marketing upcoming operas were kind of a giveaway.

The Opera de Paris, France's national opera house, was founded in 1669 by King Louis XIV as a music academy. Operas were staged at several opera houses around the city, including the Opera Garnier across the street from the Galeries Lafayette. This particular opera house was "one of the architectural masterpieces of its time." I stood across the street and took a few photos before moving on.

I mentally checked off the first item on my to-do list and proceeded to the next: the Eiffel Tower.

I descended a nearby staircase into a darkened Metro station, a city map tucked firmly in my back pocket. Using the subway was actually quite easy once you knew what you were doing, which, I supposed, was true for most things besides riding the subway, like driving a car, scrambling eggs, or having sex. The Metro wasn't unlike subways in major U.S. cities: dirty, crowded, covered in graffiti, dozens of tourists looking blankly at route maps, advertisements plastered on the walls (one notable movie poster marketed a John Travolta—Scarlett Johanssen picture "Love Song"; glowing French adjectives filling virtually every empty space; at least I think they were glowing. For all I know, it could've read "Warning! Chick Flick! Guys need not waste their money, unless on a date with a hot blonde Scandinavian, in which case you must see it immediately!").

I boarded the train, headed to what I thought was the Eiffel Tower, but realized at the first stop that I'd boarded the wrong train, although I probably would have disembarked anyway had I been on the right train. A disheveled forty-something woman with wild hair and looped earrings that could double as hula-hoops had boarded the train behind me at the previous stop, and it didn't take Sigmund Freud to see she wasn't the brightest porch light on the block.

She mumbled to herself in French, then suddenly barked at no one in particular, her tone harsh and belligerent, giving me a start (I was gazing out the window at her reflection; no way was I making eye contact). Just when I wondered whether it might be prudent to find another seat, she broke into a Cruella DeVille-like cackle and serenaded us until the train screeched to a stop at the next station.

I got off.

Calculating my extra travels had cost me fifteen minutes, I crossed the platform for the train headed in the opposite direction and boarded the correct train, soon finding myself at the Eiffel Tower station.

The Eiffel Tower is the tallest structure in Paris (1,000 feet tall) and named after its designer, Gustave Eiffel. It was the tallest structure in the world upon its completion in 1889 and remained so until 1930 when New York's Chrysler Building opened.

Before leaving the hotel, I waffled on what order I would see the sights on my only free day in Paris. Part of me wanted to first see the Eiffel Tower given the Saturday crowds but I chose otherwise. When I approached the concrete plaza beneath the tower, the long and winding path to the ticket window made my heart sink, and I lamented the wait necessary to buy a ticket, ride the elevator, take pictures, and ride back down. I stood a better chance of dating Katy Perry than ascending to the top before time ran out.

So I walked around, searching for an advance ticket booth, fingers crossed that I could fit this world-renowned monument into my schedule. I espied in the distance a ticket booth with a much shorter line. Interest piqued, I approached to find just what the travel agent ordered.

This line was for the purchase of staircase tickets. In other words, one could ascend the Eiffel Tower not by elevator (the long line) but instead by stairs. Only two of the three viewing platforms were accessible by stairs (excluding the topmost), but it mattered not to me. I immediately jumped in line and within ten minutes, I found myself bounding up an iron staircase, my wallet only four euros lighter.

As I began my ascent, I vaguely recalled Gopal mentioning something about ascending the Eiffel Tower staircase in some ridiculous length of time, but within ten minutes, I reached the first platform, about 100 feet above the ground (I could've made it in five were it not for a family of overweight Britons trudging along at a snail's pace. "I do say, Mahgret, how many bloody steps ah theh?"). I started around the narrow concourse, aiming to take pictures through the iron security fence blocking would-be suicide jumpers, but reconsidered, figuring a better view could be had from the second platform.

Another five minutes was all that separated me from the second platform. The view there was much better. One could see for miles;

words could not adequately describe the beauty and scale of the City of Love as seen from above.

I retrieved a cheap Wal-mart post-Thanksgiving-sale digital camera from my fanny pack, eager to take some snaps. I framed the perfect shot on my screen: the river Seine cutting a path through a tree-lined park surrounded by rolling hills covered by Napoleonic structures. Just as I pressed the button, the screen went blank. So I tried again.

Nothing.

The batteries had died.

Blymie!

I came all this way and was stymied by a broken down pair of double As.

I spied a tiny souvenir shop near the elevator. Entering the store, an ample supply of batteries hung from hooks behind the register. I promptly bought a four-pack, along with a few impulse buys that I couldn't resist (souvenir shops have a way of doing that). Changing the batteries did the trick, and I spent the next half hour taking pictures from all sides, snapping shots of other people so they would reciprocate in kind, taking in the incredible view, unbothered by the masses headed to the very top, where the view is probably even more spectacular, but what's an additional 800 feet when you're in a rush.

I headed across the Seine in search of the Metro, traversing the pont d'Iena bridge to the Palais de Chaillot, a palace built for an international exposition back in the late 1930's which replaced an older palace on the same spot atop a scenic hill. It presented the ideal spot to take unobstructed photos of the Eiffel Tower and, apparently, for young lovers to tongue each others' uvulas, gauging by the prevalence of couples lounging on the adjoining lawns.

The second site checked off my list, I honed my radar on the Champs-Élysées and the Arc de Triomphe.

The Arc de Triomphe is one of Paris' most recognizable monuments, a 165 foot high triumphal arch, commissioned by Napoleon in 1806 at the peak of his military career. Beneath the Arc is the Tomb of the Unknown Soldier from World War I. Many people may recognize the arc as the ending point for the annual Tour de France bike race.

As I ascended the Metro escalator to street level, the Arc gradually rose into view.

It's quite a site, a showpiece on an island, literally. It rested in the middle of a massive roundabout—or traffic circle, if you prefer (there are *lots* of those in Europe)—the intersection of multiple thoroughfares. I took a few pictures, scanning the horizon for a crosswalk, but none could be seen.

I spotted a staircase disappearing under street level. Putting two-and-two together, I realized this was how tourists could reach the Arc.

I descended the staircase and, once safely across the mighty intersection, I sought out another staircase which my AAA Tour Book said I could ascend to the top of the Arc. Seeing none, I walked around and found a ticket booth selling elevator tickets that had apparently replaced the steps and would require an 8€ payment for access (What? People would rather ride the lift than take the stairs now?). I wasn't so keen on forking over cash to reach the top, so I lingered a few minutes, taking pictures, looking around, dizzily observing cars circling the roundabout.

Returning through the tunnel brought me to the head of the Champs-Élysées, which is actually a street name (Avenue de Champs-Élysées), a tree-lined promenade that is arguably Paris' swankiest stretch of real estate (think Rodeo Drive in Hollywood). I had planned from the day's outset to eat lunch at a sidewalk café on the Champs-Élysées, not that I wanted to drop a wad in a classy bistro (they probably wouldn't have let me in anyway, my attire consisting of an untucked purple-and-white FedEx golf shirt, blue shorts, and running shoes). I simply wanted the experience, to steal a few relaxing moments before my cross-border travels to Germany in the evening.

I strolled down the wide sidewalk, past ritzy designer boutiques (Cartier, Louis Vuitton, Hugo Boss), luxurious auto show rooms (Mercedes-Benz, Peugeot—which featured futuristic sports cars in a crowded outlet, The Eagles' "There's a New Kid in Town" playing over loudspeakers), and fancy brasseries with snooty French names like Butik and McDonald's—okay, maybe not McDonald's.

My tummy grumbling, I chose a bakery and sandwich shop called Flora Danica's, mainly because it wasn't crowded and 'Danica' is the name of one of Lana's good friends and running partners, whose son is in my Cub Scout den. I figured I couldn't go wrong, oui?

Anyhow, I took a curbside table but couldn't prompt the waiter to look in my direction, even after changing tables to one with a better line of vision, or so I thought. The lack of success at a third table prompted me to go inside and order from their pre-made selections. I chose a smoked salmon sandwich as long as my arm, a cold Heineken, and a mouth-watering dessert called a Kringle-chocolat, a triangular glazed pastry which oozed so much chocolate I wanted to jump over the counter and kiss the lady cashier for selling such a delectable treat.

I returned outside and sat at one of the tables, eating my sandwich one bite at a time from a plastic sleeve. I learned by watching others that the French eat their sandwiches not by removing them from the sleeves and tearing off chunks with their teeth but instead sliding back the sleeve to expose a corner of the sandwich before tearing off chunks with their teeth. The weather was Spring-like—expansive sunny blue skies, a pleasantly cool breeze taking the edge off the heat—and a steady stream of passers-by filled the sidewalk, a mix of dialects forming a patchwork global language.

I was about to dig into my Kringle when a waitress approached. In pleasant French, she began with "Excusez-moi, monsieur . . ." and I knew immediately that my time at the table had ended.

I suspected an employee might object to my eating take-out food at an outside table. It wasn't like I bought take-out from, say, McDonald's (which was a few doors down). I mean, I was eating their food after all. I just didn't buy it outside. Nevertheless, I found a neglected table in the corner near the front and hoped they wouldn't notice.

They did.

I immediately responded to the inquiry with a contrite "Oui, Oui" and collected my things, although I must say it was the most pleasant experience I've ever had being booted. It didn't matter what she said; it was how she said it: smiling, pleasant almost apologetic tone, lilting French that flowed so romantically from her lips I would've gladly responded to any command. For all I knew, she could've said, "Excuse me, sir, but I'm going to cut your family into tiny pieces and feed them to my iguana," and I would've leapt up, saluting a response, "Oui! Oui, Mademoiselle!"

It didn't matter anyway. One glance at my clip-on clock revealed the time to be 2:00 p.m.

Cut-off time.

I consumed the Kringle on the way to the Metro and rode a maze of connecting trains to the airport, where I caught a shuttle to the hotel, retrieved my bags, and made the same journey in reverse, stopping at the Gare du Nord train station, arriving over 90 minutes early for my departure (I wasn't about to cut it close again!).

I wasted an hour in a brasserie adjacent to the platforms, nursing a Foster's, checking in with Lana on my cell, a steady stream of PA announcements preceded by a pithy melody that reminded me of the first four notes of Bon Jovi's "You Give Love a Bad Name" ("Shot through the heart . . ."). Boarding began fifteen minutes before departure and I was one of the first to have my ticket punched.

The TGV from Paris to Cologne ('Koln' in French) would take four hours, with stops in Brussels, Liege and Aachen. I spent the time writing, eating dinner, and gazing out the window at the incredible countryside, an expressway running parallel to the track, the train zooming past autos speeding in excess of 110 km/hr but looking as though propelled by a child.

We arrived a few minutes early at the Cologne train station. I tried calling the hotel on my cell to ask for a shuttle bus, but couldn't get through (I must have written their number down wrong), so I hailed a taxi, which took only five minutes to deliver me safe and sound.

Upon arrival, I first thought I'd been driven to the wrong place. Two men wearing black suits stood guard at the entrance, a long tongue of red carpet extended from the curb to beneath a black sheet shielding the door, velvet ropes lined the path. Two women showed their IDs to the men, who pulled back a corner of the sheet, allowing them entry. Either this hotel went to a lot of trouble to make me feel welcome or my reservation was at Studio 54.

Once inside, the lobby resembled a club in the hours before business picked up. Disoriented by blaring dance music and bright colored spotlights, my vision blurred from an abundance of machine smoke. I had to ask twice whether I was in the right place and was assured each time that I was.

I almost couldn't find the front desk; it sat on the edge of the fray. The exchanges with the desk clerk consisted of yelling "What?" a lot, cupping my good ear to capture his words, immediately lost in the din of music and conversations. I asked about the revelry and she explained it was a monthly party for the over 30 set, though by the sight of things there weren't many thirty-somethings in Cologne, as only a handful of men and women stood at chest-high bar tables, sipping aperitifs, and looking more or less indifferent.

I was glad to get my key and retire to the silence of my room. It was a nice hotel (a European chain called Sofitel), conveniently located across the Rhine River from the Cologne business district, only a short jog away.

I checked email for a while but a thought kept nagging at me, reflections of Gopal telling me to loosen up and live a little. I'd planned to stay in my room for the balance of the evening (it was about 10:00 p.m. at the time) but instead chose to go downstairs and join in the fun. So I donned nicer clothes and descended the elevator to the lobby.

I could feel the bass thumping in my chest long before the elevator doors opened, and the scene it revealed had completely transformed from what I'd found only a half-hour earlier.

The lobby was crammed with people, standing shoulder-to-shoulder, in small groups and alone on the fringes, leaning into each other's ears for short bursts of conversation, a core of females dancing in the center to a Madonna tune. I pushed my way through the mob, in the direction of a bar in the adjacent room, but found more of the same crowd packed tightly like a bound stack of newspapers. My enthusiasm dwindled with every forced step as the setting represented everything I hated about being single.

I made a loop around and returned to my room, offering a silent prayer for my wife, filling the rest of my night with email, Internet surfing, writing, and TV, before retiring for bed after 1:00 a.m.

Auf Wiedersehen (that's 'good bye' in German).

The Eiffel Tower, one of the world's most recognizable structures.

The author posing at the Arc de Triomphe monument.

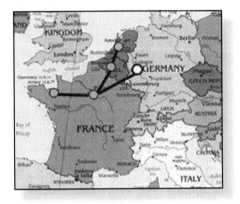

Chapter 4

Spontaneous Germany

Webster's Online Dictionary defines 'spontaneous' as "proceeding from natural feeling or native tendency without external constraint" or "arising from a momentary impulse." I've been thinking a lot about this word as I reflected on my first full day in Cologne, but I'm getting ahead of myself.

It pleased me greatly to sleep until I could sleep no more, awaking at 9:30 a.m., having an unhurried breakfast, although one must keep an eye on the waiters. I arose to refill my orange juice glass and when I returned to the table, not ninety seconds later, my plate had disappeared.

Before returning to my room, I asked a desk clerk for a city map, adding that I'm a runner and would like a guide to take with me.

He began to hand over a larger folded map but paused upon hearing the word "runner", offering instead a special map for runners, a smaller detailed map of Cologne, folded neatly into the size of a credit card, solid and dotted red lines (for jogging and skating routes, respectively) extending from a red dot marking the hotel toward a park and other paths lining either side of the Rhine River.

I quickly changed into my running clothes and—map in hand, fanny pack secured around my waist—headed away from the Dorint Sofitel An Der Messe Koln and into the unknown wonders of Cologne.

It took a while before I found the path to Rhein Park, first hitting a dead end on a long warehouse road (I yelled "Rhein Park?" at a parking lot attendant, pointing in the direction I thought led me to the park, but he responded by shrugging his shoulders). I doubled back and followed the main thoroughfare in the opposite direction (against my map's advice), soon finding a welcoming expanse of green adjacent to a tall tubular gray building and split by an asphalt path, easily identifiable as ingress to the park.

The path led up a slow incline toward the Hohenzollern Bridge, a train bridge spanning the Rhine and somewhat resembling the I-40 Bridge in Memphis (the "M" bridge, as my boys call it), its middle hump rising above the two on either side. I paused to take a picture of the scenic Cologne skyline before dashing across the bridge's pedestrian walkway.

Upon reaching the downtown side, I descended stairs to the riverfront and headed away from the bridge. The concrete-stoned sidewalk teemed with tourists and locals enjoying a mid-day stroll under bright sunny skies, bike riders weaving through the pedestrian traffic, large planters choked with weeds on my left, a slight smell of fish wafting from the Rhine on my right. The river abounded with commerce: barges chugging along, forcing large loads against the brisk current, cruisers jammed with camera-toting tourists motoring in both directions.

I turned around at the Zoobrucke—another bridge. I occasionally passed sweaty runners—running bibs pinned to their shirts and race medals hung around their necks—walking in the opposite direction. I figured a road race must have been held that morning, silently sorrowful at missing a running opportunity.

I passed under the Hohenzollern Bridge, headed south toward the Deutzer Bridge, when the crowd density thickened, a barricade splitting the sidewalk in two. Most of the crowd navigated the river side, so I ducked under the tape and ran on the more open side, occupied by bikers and runners, but in fewer numbers.

After a half mile or so, I encountered more runners with race bibs, and figured I was headed in the direction of the finish line, running in the lane reserved for racers.

But the crowds continued to swell, spectators lining the temporary barricade, facing my direction, clapping, offering German words of encouragement, and a smidgen of suspicion welled up inside me that perhaps they were cheering for me.

Block after block, the path narrowed, compressed on both sides by cheering masses, their deafening applause kick-starting my adrenaline. I turned a hairpin corner, crossed a steel bridge with green and white balloons strung in an arc across the top, and, inspired by the raucous ovation, raised my arms, smiling, high-fiving hands extended over the barricades. My pace—not to mention my heart rate—quickened when the finish line came into view, and I crossed it triumphantly, a race clock showing 2 hours and 21 minutes, in which case I'd either knocked two hours off my best marathon time or ran the slowest 5K in world history.

The after-party had begun a while ago, judging by the volume of trash on the ground: banana peels, empty beer bottles, crushed plastic cups, energy bar wrappers. At first, having no race bib elevated my self-consciousness, but no one seemed to care. I was dressed as a runner, melding with the sweaty throng, not immediately identifiable as a party crasher.

I checked my watch and estimated I'd been running almost an hour—covering between five and six miles, three miles short of my intended distance, but I couldn't resist the opportunity to join the post-race partying, satisfied runners gleaming with perspiration, earsplitting music broadcast over loudspeakers, broken occasionally by PA announcements in German ("Achtung! In veenigan minooten aahtsen beeten"; at least, that's what it sounded like).

The remaining miles could wait.

I grabbed water first, downing a few cups before making headway to the beer. From behind a ring of picnic tables, a half-dozen winded young men struggled to keep up with the demand for a German brand called Erlanger. I waited a few minutes before obtaining a large cup, a thick head of foam oozing over the sides. I ate a few energy bars while waiting for the foam to evaporate, but wasn't entirely satisfied with its thin and unfulfilling taste, so I tossed it in the garbage (I learned later it was non-alcoholic beer).

Later, I happened upon a large bulletin board on which race results had been tacked on 8x11 sheets of paper. It was then I learned that the race distance had been 15.2 km, or about 9.5 miles. I reflected silently that it was good I had no race chip recording an official time because I would've been sorely disappointed with a 2:21 finish time in a 15K race (almost a 15 minute-mile pace).

I lingered a while, delaying the inevitable departure, the remaining three miles looming over me like a headache. Walking toward the steel bridge I had crossed prior to "finishing", neither my head nor legs desired resuming a run, given the forty-five minute break. I ignored a nagging itch to start again, loitering instead in the post-race area, ambling through a nearby museum displaying sports memorabilia of German Olympians, full of autographed soccer balls, bronzed moldings of people's feet, and an expansive wing honoring Max Schmeling, World Heavyweight boxing champion in the early 30's and self-proclaimed Aryan Superman who lunched with Hitler and had lengthy conversations with Goebbels, master propagandist of the Nazi regime.

Eventually, I had to leave, so I resigned myself to another half-hour of running, but first I would remain downtown and pursue a suitable site for lunch. I was about to take my first stride when the wind shifted, carrying with it the glorious aroma of cooked meat. My nose followed the trail of smoke to its source: a carnival-like food trailer with the word "bratwurst" featured prominently on the sides.

I knew then I was done running for the day.

I waited in line fifteen minutes to place my order: a single bratwurst, plain, no kraut. For the measly sum of two euros, the cook returned a steaming, juicy bratwurst, placed inside what looked like an O'Charley's dinner roll, which could barely contain the length of the foot-long brat. I squeezed a generous amount of spicy mustard down its length before starting down the riverside path, eating as I walked, savoring every bite.

With no running on the horizon, I thought it time to switch into tourist mode. The riverfront scene bustled with activity: lovers sunning in the mid-day warmth (a bank listed the temperature at 17 Celsius, about 62 Fahrenheit), diners lingering at sidewalk tables. I had seen a church steeple rising above the nearby buildings and headed in that direction.

The church of Groß St. Martin has been a prominent fixture of Cologne's old town since the Middle Ages. The church was closed, but I read that the Spanish, Portuguese and Philippine communities in Cologne used the church for their services earlier in the day.

My next destination was perhaps Cologne's most visible and striking structure: the Cologne Cathedral. One of Germany's best known architectural monuments, the cathedral was the second tallest Gothic structure in the world and took over 600 years to complete when construction finally ended in 1880.

On the inside, its scale was as impressive as its exterior, massive stained glass windows, gothic arches that stretched toward the clouds. Arguably the most celebrated work of art in the cathedral was the Sarcophagus of the Magi, a large gilded sarcophagus dating from the 13th century, and the largest reliquary, or holy relic container, in the Western world. The shrine was a decorated triple sarcophagus placed above and behind the high altar of the cathedral. It reportedly contained the bones of the Three Wise Men.

Also there were numerous ornate burial crypts topped by curious sculptures representing the deceased person in repose (the oldest I saw dated to the 1370's).

Leaving the cathedral, I navigated a maze of streets, surveying sidewalk menus for possible dinner options, stopping once to buy a bottle of water to quench my thirst while window-shopping on a busy street lined with kitschy souvenir shops. At one corner, I spied the Museum Ludwig, figuring it must have something to do with the composer Ludwig von Beethoven, whom I knew lived in Germany. As I crossed a street toward the museum, squeals of adolescent girls filled my ears.

Curious about the commotion, I found a high spot to see over a construction site and glimpsed a horde of teenage girls—'teenagers' being a safe assumption given the last time I heard a thirty-something woman scream was when I forgot to leave the toilet seat down—crowded around a green van blocking a hotel entrance. Curious to know what was going on, I bypassed the construction and approached the hotel.

The scene reminded me of something out of an Elvis documentary. Dozens of screaming girls, all waving arms and frenzied shrieks, jockeyed to position themselves for autographs from what looked like two boys (all I could see was their black baseball caps above the tussle). Suddenly, the mass shifted to the right as a security guard struggled to keep the admirers at bay. The boys approached the van and hopped inside, the guard slamming the door behind them, but the fans wouldn't be deterred, sneaking pictures through the dark tinted glass, hopping on the front bumper for an unobstructed photo op through the windshield. It took a few minutes for the van to pull away, and those devotees who'd managed to get an autograph or picture hugged each other, bouncing giddily.

The whole scene made me want to stick a finger down my throat.

But I had to know who the famous people were.

Two girls walked past me speaking English and I asked about the boys. She told me but I didn't understand, not that she spoke poor English but more likely that I'm woefully out of touch with most things popular.

"What?" I barked, pushing forward the back of my ear.

She told me again, but I still didn't get it.

"I'm sorry but I'm an old guy who knows nothing about these things. May I?" I gestured to a poster folded in her hand. She stretched it out, revealing four adolescent boys posed in stylish teenage fashion, basically the disheveled look.

The words "Tokio Hotel" at the bottom finally gave me the answer to my question.

"This one's my favorite," added one girl, pointing to an androgynous-looking boy and I indulged her with an indifferent smile.

"Are you from the States?"

It was an innocent question. Her English so well articulated that I drew the only logical conclusion, in my mind anyway.

"Uh, no," she retorted, regarding me with a "As if . . ." raised-eyebrow look, and I knew then that I'd reinforced the universal myth harbored by teenagers all over the world that adults don't know squat about anything.

The time approaching 2:00 p.m., I started back to my hotel, deciding to run those final three miles en route. By the time I returned, I'd added nearly four miles, contentedly jogging on the eastern bank of the Rhine, through the riverfront Rhine Park, full of parents pushing strollers and sweeping lawns busy with games of soccer. I was satisfied with reaching my desired mileage, albeit broken by some of the most spontaneous fun I'd ever had.

I spent the next two hours at the hotel, showering, writing, waiting for housekeeping to clean my room.

I had no idea where I'd eat dinner—no menu caught my eye enough to take notice—but I was undeterred, setting out a little after five to walk back to the downtown area.

Cologne is remarkably pedestrian-friendly, the central business district a maze of cobbled streets lined with a variety of restaurants and shops (mostly closed given it was Sunday). I wandered from block to block, studying dozens of menus, finding few bilingual ones, reluctant to patronize any that didn't have English translations, for it would be just my luck to try something new and order "schwinerückensteak", for no other reason than 'steak' looked familiar, and get served a dish of pan fried sheep's tongue with a side of baked cow utters in a minty béarnaise sauce (actually, schwinerückensteak is pork steak with mushroom sauce).

After a half-hour of wandering, I arrived at the plaza facing the Cologne Cathedral, and noticed a small crowd surrounding a street performer. As I neared, an alluring high-pitched flute cut through the air, drawing me closer.

A four-foot tall black man held court, sunglasses perched atop his short afro, expertly blowing into a wooden flute while simultaneously creating a beat by rocking from one foot to the other, small cymbals attached to his shoes, one under the right heel, the other under the left toe, his tunes so joyful and rhythmic that the burgeoning crowd couldn't help but tap their collective feet in unison.

I paused for ten minutes, forgetting my hunger pangs, enthralled by the man's captivating tunes, one morphing into the next, an uninterrupted performance delivered with such aptitude that it prompted me to do something spontaneous.

I gave him money.

I wasn't the only one, mind you. His collection bucket—which resembled an upturned half-coconut—had already been plentifully supplied, but I felt compelled to contribute; it would've been disrespectful to linger so long and depart without showing at least some appreciation for the performance.

Other street performers were scattered about the plaza, many wearing silly costumes—Spiderman and Mata Hari, among others—and standing still, frozen curiosities atop metal boxes. I'm probably not that still when I sleep, so perhaps there's some talent involved, but it's unfair to place them in the same category with the flute player, akin to liking Michael Jordan's athletic talents with, say, mine.

I strolled from the plaza, extra buoyancy in my step, and resumed my quest for dinner, the blissful echo of a wooden flute fading into the void, a broad smile spanning my face.

After another half-hour of nomadic drifting, led by impulse alone, I arrived at an attention-grabbing square—called Heumarkt; two blocks west of the Rhine near where the Deutzer Bridge crossed—surrounded by a wide selection of eateries, and I made up my mind to select one of its options.

I chose Memo's Restaurant and Bar, whose bilingual menu sealed the deal. I took a seat at a long wooden sidewalk table, beneath a Kelly green umbrella branded with the name of a German beer. Curiously mounted on the restaurant façade was a small brown UPS logo (a gift from UPS pilots who often ate there, I would learn later).

I noticed many people drinking the beer whose brand was prominently displayed on the umbrella shading me from the afternoon sun, so I ordered a tall glass of Gilden Kölsch. Scanning the menu, I ordered the most intriguing option—rumpsteak—mainly because I'd seen it on many menus and figured it must be a German specialty. The waitress—server, food attendant, whatever—asked me if I wanted it cooked medium. Normally, I order meat medium-well as it's my preference, not to mention it doesn't bleed all over the plate, but in a spontaneous moment, I asked if that's how she recommended it. She said, yes, it was better that way.

So that's how I ordered it.

I must add that while I like steak, I rarely order it in restaurants (and rarely 'rarely'—haha). As I sat at the table, the uncomfortable wooden slats of my chair cutting into my legs, a stiff breeze flapping the umbrella over my head, I couldn't remember the last time I ordered steak while dining out.

When it arrived, the steak concealed most of the plate, the exposed fraction occupied by a generous serving of frites, or fries. It must have weighed eight ounces, enough to split with a partner and with plenty left over. I hadn't planned to eat the whole thing, but its savory spices kept inviting me to have another bite, and I didn't stop until all that remained was a plate of half-eaten frites soaked in steak blood.

I would've eaten dessert but passed due to being overly stuffed, my arms too tired to lift anything further to my mouth. I tottered back to the hotel, suitably satisfied, content to waste away the evening writing (which kept my mind off of wasting away from too much dinner), my television tuned to a U.S. Open tennis match, broadcast in German.

"Wimmern! Ein was für ausgezeichneter Schuß durch Andy Roddick! (This is what Dictionary.com says is the German translation for, "Wow! What an excellent shot by Andy Roddick!")

I reflected on the day, driven largely by spontaneity and impulse. My predictability is well-known in my family and small circle of friends. Most days, I'm about as spontaneous as the sunrise. But on this day, perhaps I made a breakthrough. Maybe I'll become a new person, more care-free and unstructured, more willing to take risks, more likely to suppress my native tendency for internal constraint and live life on impulse.

Naaaaaahhhh.

Autobahn is the German word for a major high-speed road, similar to a freeway in English-speaking countries. The big difference being that stretches of German autobahns have no speed limit (though about 50% of the total length is subject to local and/or conditional limits), but the "recommended speed" is 130 km/h (80 mph).

I spent the following morning with a tall, handsome, balding German named Hans, who led me on a customer sales call to a charming mountain town called Lüdenscheid. (I thought we were going to an intriguingly-named town called "Ausfahrt", as that's what the directional sign read as we exited the highway, but I learned later that "ausfahrt" means "exit" in German). Later, he handed me over to one of his colleagues, Leo, a goateed man of Portuguese heritage living in Germany. Leo led me to his navy blue Ford Mondeo diesel mini station wagon for an hour's drive to a West German town called Oelde.

Roughly halfway into our journey, past rolling hillocks covered with impenetrable evergreens and terraced towns perched precariously on sloping hillsides, a gradual acceleration slowly pressed me into my seat and, in the middle of a conversation about the European competitive market, I stole a glance at the speedometer.

140 km/hr.

Leo shifted into fourth gear.

A moment later: 160 km/hr.

The conversation continued.

Fifth gear.

180 km/hr.

"So, um, what do you think about UPS?" I asked with an edge in my voice.

190 km/hr.

Wow! I thought. *I'm really on the Autobahn!*

Sixth gear.

200 km/hr.

210 km/hr.

The speedometer topped out at 220 km/hr before Leo slowed the car as we approached a speed zone (frankly, I didn't know a Ford could go that fast!). I was so excited I struggled to focus on the conversation and complete quick math in my head to convert the speed into miles per hour (it's about 137 mph).

(I learned later that Gopal's Autobahn experience topped mine, his host reaching 240 km/hr, or just shy of 150 mph).

It reminded me of a time during my senior year in college, not long after a new car purchase (a 1989 black Olds Cutlass Supreme). I drove a roommate, who lived near my hometown, east on I-40, returning to the Vanderbilt campus after a weekend visiting our respective families. Stalled traffic just shy of the Tennessee River prompted me to detour north on the Camden highway. Emboldened by my new car, curious to test its capabilities, and perhaps egged on by my roommate, I waited for a flat stretch and put the pedal to the metal, both of us howling with excitement as we watched the digital speedometer accelerate, reaching 100 mph before I slowed down.

I never did it again; not in that car nor any other I've owned since.

Okay, I may have been a bit disconcerted riding in a car going 137 mph, but it was more exhilarating than scary. Leo said that there are stretches of rural highway throughout Germany that qualified as

'Autobahn' expressways, when, as he put it, you could "go for free", which meant no speed limit.

I mentioned how thrilling it was to go so fast, which seemed to amuse him. Dense traffic precluded further speeds in excess of 200 km/hr, but we managed to sustain velocities of about 180 km/hr (roughly 112 mph) where allowed.

Our work day ended around 4:30 p.m., and it took us nearly an hour and a half to reach Ratingen, a suburb of Düsseldorf, with a stop in Dortmund in between. My hotel, the Holiday Inn Düsseldorf Airport—Ratingen, was a bland, drab two-story structure, constructed in a style that I thought went out with hoop skirts and bouffant hairdos. Spoiled by stays in four-star hotels since my arrival in Europe, I felt like a man whose Armani suit had been switched with a seersucker coat.

My stomach growled for sustenance as I'd skipped lunch and had nothing to eat since breakfast except for a Werther's caramel Leo offered before our last sales call. My proximity to the airport offered little hope in finding an eatery within walking distance, but instead of holing up in my room, wallowing in self-pity, I slipped into my shoes and headed out for a stroll. But deciding which way to go would not be easy.

The hotel sat at the point of a three-way intersection. Looking left at the traffic light, a shady tree-lined road disappeared into the horizon, not a structure in sight. Looking right, a chain link fence marked a desolate stretch of airport boundary. Straight ahead, locals walking the sidewalk provided a modicum of optimism, so I headed east on Berliner Straße, or Berlin Street (the ß is a German character representing a double S—Strasse meaning "street").

Twenty minutes of walking led me into a residential neighborhood, lined by tall high rise apartment buildings painted in a variety of curious colors (mauve, ruby red, Tennessee orange), residents milling about, riding bikes, parents carefully watching over children on a playground, a father and son playing street hockey in a cul-de-sac.

But still no restaurants in sight.

I did, however, spot an Aldi grocery store, a popular German chain I recognized from a store near my Memphis office. Unexcited about the prospect of having dinner in the hotel restaurant, I resigned myself to a ready-made sandwich in the grocery store.

Aldi possessed a warehouse feel about it, but not because it was a large metal box with exposed trusses and racks of food in large servings.

Instead, it had a spartan look, with wide aisles and meager offerings, boxes of food stacked on the floor, no apparent logic to its order (chocolate sold next to the wine, being one example). I grabbed a bag of chips and a package of Granada milk chocolate (vollmilch-schokolade) cookies before searching for a sandwich.

One look at the sandwiches turned my stomach; it reminded me of what you might buy at a vending machine: twin layers of thin mystery meat lathered with mayo between slices of stale white bread. I immediately bypassed the sandwiches and returned the chips before leaving the store (but not without buying the cookies).

Returning to the moroseness of the inn, I dreaded dinner in the hotel bistro, reluctantly entering, asking for a table for one, and was led to a non-smoking table near a family of three, a charming blonde-haired toddler entertaining his mom and dad—and the solo gentleman dining alone next to them—with a series of incomprehensible sounds that only parents can understand.

I ordered penne pasta drowning in a creamy white gorgonzola cheese sauce, which was actually quite good, the portion size so hefty I wondered if I'd mistakenly ordered for two. I tried to clean the plate but my distended stomach wouldn't accept another bite, so it was with a satisfied grunt I pushed away from the table and returned to my room for the evening, desiring to watch TV before retiring to bed, but it wasn't working—the TV, not the bed—though I managed to fix it (the cable input had come unplugged). I then tried to call home but the phone wasn't working. So it was with distaste in my mouth that I tucked myself into bed, facetiously wondering what I might find wrong with my room in the morning.

It would be the shower.

I consider myself a smart guy—if, that is, I'm allowed to count the college of useless knowledge occupying valuable brain cells, like the license plate of JFK's assassination limo (GG-300) and who won the National League batting title in 1985 (Willie McGee)—but, for the life of me, I couldn't figure out how to turn on the shower. I pushed, pulled and twisted everything that seemed logical, but nothing worked (I can now completely assemble a bath and shower spigot, if you ever need a plumber). It was a shame really, not just because my underarms smelled like rotten fruit but because I really wanted a long, hot shower that cleared the cobwebs from my head, particularly when my last three hours of sleep had been continually interrupted with what I thought in my semi-consciousness was a next-door neighbor intermittently cranking up the TV volume but actually were low-flying planes departing the airport.

Tuesday morning brought more sales calls: in the morning with a diminutive short-tempered salesman named Markus and the afternoon with a long-haired brunette named Claudia who had recently rejoined the company after a three-year maternity leave (U.S. companies should be so generous!). At the end of a long day, after driving hundreds of kilometers visiting customer locations in beautiful West German towns, Claudia passed me off to a Global Account Manager named Roland, a brawny goateed man with curly salt and pepper hair and a disarming sense of humor.

Roland's job was to drive me from the FedEx station in Cologne to my hotel in Ratingen, which was near his home and would save Claudia from driving out of her way.

Before taking me to my hotel, speeding down a highway leading away from Cologne, he wanted to show me something. We exited the highway ("Ausfahrt!") and followed a winding valley road, dense trees concealing the hills on both sides.

He soon pulled the car into the parking lot of a small but breath-taking cathedral in a valley clearing. He said that this cathedral—the Altenberg Cathedral—dated to the 1100s and possessed the largest stained-glass window in the country.

It was founded as a monastery in 1133 and since 1857 had been simultaneously used as a church by Catholic as well as Protestant Christians. Once inside, Roland pointed out that its interior closely resembled the Cologne Cathedral, though on a much smaller scale.

I stood at the back of the apse and photographed the colorful west window (finished before 1397), which was indeed the largest medieval church window preserved in Germany; it showed saints standing in two rows, occupying the scenery of the Heavenly Jerusalem, angel musicians and the four Fathers of the Church in the tracery above.

Suddenly the pipe organ came to life, and for a moment I thought I'd been transported into an old haunted house movie—chilling chords resonated throughout the church; grand acoustics giving the impression of a majestic organ but I found it to be no more impressive than those in a modern American sanctuary.

After lighting a candle below a gilded sculpture—of the Virgin Mary, I think—we departed the sanctuary, Roland recalling visits to the church in his youth, gracefully waiting as I ducked into the gift shop to buy postcards for my niece, who collected them and was studying the continents in school.

As we pulled from the lot, gravel crunching under the tires of his Mercedes-Benz, he asked if I was hungry. For the second day in a row I had skipped lunch, so "famished" best described my appetite.

"Good," he said, "what do you like to eat?"

"I'm pretty much a meat and potatoes guy."

"Do you drink beer?"

"Ya." (This had become my new favorite word. It wasn't just a word of affirmation but also came in handy to break uncomfortable silences or confirm you were paying attention).

"I know just the place."

Fifteen minutes later, we found ourselves at a Dom Kölschgarten, a beer pub for a brand of Cologne beer called Dom, situated on a busy street corner in Roland's hometown of Leverkusen.

According to my AAA Tour Book, the Cologne area had two dozen breweries, more than any other German city. All produced the local beer, or Kölsch, which was light and clear and served in tall, slim glasses. Roland ordered us two Kölsches, which arrived as we pondered the menu—actually, Roland did most of the pondering as it was printed completely in German; I just wondered.

"A toast . . ." he blurted, smiling, raising his Kölsch to me. He then said something in German, which I tried to repeat phonetically as I touched my glass to his, but he suddenly pulled his away.

"My eyes," he said, and I thought he was having a problem with his eyes. Roland made a 'V' with his index and ring fingers and looked as though he would poke himself in the eyes, but he then explained, "In Germany, we look each other in the eyes when we make a toast."

Oh, okay.

So we tried again, and I looked him square in the eyes as I repeated his toast and we clinked our glasses together.

He insisted on ordering for me, wanting me to experience a real German meal. I felt at ease as he consulted with me on several selections he thought would fit my tastes before placing the order with the waiter in German.

For starters, we ate a soup called Risenbockwurst, similar to a beef stew with chunks of meat and potatoes but in a spicy broth. For my entrée, I thoroughly enjoyed nürnburger rostbratwürstchen, a juicy smoked sausage topped with mustard with a side of pommes (round sliced potatoes) and sauerkraut, which to Roland's delight I actually enjoyed (this after previously explaining that I disliked kraut).

We took pleasure in a long dinner and leisurely conversation that spanned a sunset peeking through old-growth trees. Roland amused me with travel stories in the half-hour drive to my hotel, where he dropped me off with a firm handshake and well wishes for my remaining travels.

Gopal and I reunited over dinner in the hotel restaurant—he ate, I drank water—before I excused myself at the serving of his entrée, retiring to my room for packing and writing, amused by "Grey's Anatomy" dubbed in German on the TV. I didn't understand a word of it, but it didn't stop me from dubbing my own dialogue over the familiar scenes and incomprehensible German chatter, particularly when you're bored out of your gourd.

For example: "Ah, Herr George. Wan dam de nahck les shtad ze gahdren hoffen" means "Ah, George. Is that a colon in your pocket or are you just glad to see me?"

Don't say I haven't learned anything on my travels!

The Cologne Cathedral rises over the Rhine River. It is one of Germany's best known architectural monuments and dates to the 13th Century.

*Cologne residents and tourists enjoy a sunny day
in a park fronting the Rhine River.*

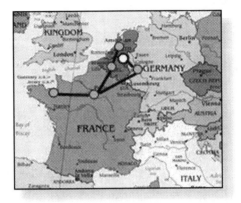

CHAPTER 5

Return to the Netherlands

As I rode a 7:09 a.m. train, low-hanging clouds glowed in the sunrise. Facing another cross-border journey, my seventh hotel check-in on the horizon, I reflected how what remained of my trip resembled a silver platter sitting neglected in a china cabinet.

The luster had gone.

Rarely had I looked so forward to ending a trip, the trappings of home luring me like a magnet. So much of the early enthusiasm had eroded, like a river eating into its banks, slowly, deliberately, invisible to the naked eye, its forces at work beneath the surface.

I found the extensive breakfast buffets less alluring, the beds less comfortable, the taxis and trains more a burden than an adventure, the task of remembering my room number more challenging, the restaurants more stale (from familiarity, not quality).

I was ready to go home.

The German segment had drained my energy like a punctured tire.

The Germans had such determination and focus! They drove hundreds of square kilometers covering vast sales territories, worked through lunch, and scheduled two-hour noontime meetings, scarcely taking breaks in between (except for one escort, who bypassed lunch yet was compelled to pull over on a shady industrial road for a five-minute smoke break). If I hadn't stuffed the remaining grocery store cookies in my briefcase when checking out of the hotel, I would've had no mid-day sustenance for three days.

Returning to the Netherlands offered a reprieve. Eindhoven was a city in the south of Holland, about 200,000 people (fifth largest in the country) founded in 1232 at the confluence of two streams, only one of which still remains (the Dommel). Large-scale air raids in World War II (including the preliminary bombing during Operation Market Garden to aid paratroopers in securing the bridges in and around the town) destroyed large parts of the city. The reconstruction that followed left very little historical remains, so while it maintained the Dutch small-town charm I'd come to savor, it lacked the historical impressiveness of other European cities.

After arriving late in the day in Eindhoven via train, Gopal and I settled in before walking to an Indian restaurant—A Taste of India (perhaps the best Indian meal I've ever had: curry fish lightly spiced over a bed of rice with a side of lentil-flavored potatoes)—a few blocks south of our hotel, my second Dorint Sofitel stay on this tour, a European hotel I highly recommend. It was a bit on the pricey side but I found it clean, comfortable, and well-located. It also had a feature I'd never seen before: small recessed lighting in the ceiling above the door that projected the room number on the floor. Room numbers were also posted on the wall, but it was cool to walk its halls and spy your room number stenciled in light on the floor.

Thursday brought another sales call with an international giant. Philips is one of the largest electronics companies in the world and was founded in Eindhoven in 1891 by brothers Gerard and Anton Philips as a light bulb factory. It was Eindhoven's biggest employer and contributed to the local economy in a similar fashion to FedEx in Memphis, perhaps more so.

Its headquarters was a sprawling campus on a flat plain in the southern part of the city. Acres of open, airy lawns and rippling lakes teeming with ducks surrounded dozens of buildings. When Gopal and I arrived with Ann the Local and a FedEx Global Sales Rep named Gillian—an auburn-haired Briton whose height and size dwarfed us all—for a lunch meeting with Gillian's Philips contact, the grounds were abuzz with activity, many of the company's 8,000 employees strolled to and from an expansive cafeteria, jogged around the perimeter road, and bought foodstuffs at an on-site market. It wasn't a bad place to work.

After a two-hour lunch meeting, we asked the lady from Philips for advice about evening activities in Eindhoven. She was a razor-sharp executive who spoke excellent English but, perhaps because English wasn't her first language, often verbalized her punctuation while speaking. For example, she said, "So I would ask you about the competition, so to say, and why they might in brackets attempt to launch new services in this market question mark?"

"Ah, Eindhoven?" she asked, quizzically, her pitch elevated an octave, as if to say, *"Why would you want to stay in Eindhoven?"*

She suggested we catch a train and travel south an hour to a town called Maastricht. There we would find plenty of restaurants and shopping, much better than in Eindhoven.

We had just enough time at the hotel following our afternoon meetings to quickly cast our suits on the bed, make a Superman-esque change into more comfortable clothes, briskly walk to the central station near our hotel, and buy two round-trip train tickets to Maastricht.

I have absolutely fallen in love with train travel. It's a shame that America hasn't made train travel more convenient—or at least better marketed the services—but so goes our car-loving culture. In Europe, not only is train travel convenient, it's affordable. Gopal and I spent less on a two-hour round trip train ticket than a thirty-minute cab ride in the city. No bumper-to-bumper traffic. No driving stresses. One need only kick back with a book, iPod or sudoku puzzle, or stare out the window at the postcard panoramas. The stresses of train riding were few and far between.

I passed the hour to Maastricht finishing my Bill Bryson travel book, a refreshing breeze blowing in through an open window, though I was often startled when gazing absentmindedly at vistas of lush green fields bordered by manicured hedgerows when—

THWOOOSH!!

A blast of air from a passing train roused me from my trance, a blur of steel and glass, gone as swiftly as it arrived.

The Maastricht station was constructed in a style that one expected of train stations: iron columns supporting wide canopies that protect elevated platforms of checkered concrete stones, brick façades and arched windows that evoked an era of steam trains and derby hats. Outside, hundreds of bikes were parked neatly in a corner near the main entrance, and the visceral charm of the Netherlands made it my favorite stop on this whirlwind tour.

Maastricht is a small city of 120,000 people straddling the Meuse River in southeastern Holland, situated between Belgium and Germany. It is arguably the oldest city in the country—Old Stone Age remains have been found to the west of the city—and Celts lived here at least 500 years before the Romans arrived. Maastricht was the first Dutch city liberated by the Allies in World War II, and the Maastricht Treaty was signed there in 1992, leading to the creation of the Euro.

Gopal and I selected an avenue perpendicular to the train station to begin our search for a suitable dining establishment. We soon crossed the Saint Servatius bridge—the oldest in Maastricht—a scenic overpass spanning the Meuse River, and arrived at a central district with narrow cobbled walkways, inviting restaurants, and, to our surprise, countless shops still open for business (unlike America, most European shops close around sunset). We wandered about, taking advantage of photo ops that presented themselves—ancient cathedrals, winding streets abutted by fetching homes. Natives milled about, some picking french fries from what looked like upturned traffic cones and concealed by a viscous layer of mayonnaise and ketchup.

We selected from one of many restaurants on the scenic Vrijthof, a picturesque cathedral at one end of an spacious square, a fetching eatery named La Brasserie Monopole calling out to us, 'Heineken Bier' in giant neon lettering above the entrance. We took a street-front table beneath wide umbrellas amid hundreds of diners. I washed down my codfish filets in lobster sauce with a couple of Heinekens, adding yet another succulent meal to the litany of others I'd consumed thus far.

By the time we boarded the train for our return trip to Eindhoven, night had fallen, and the codfish fillets had made a beeline through my digestive system, not uncommon given my finicky stomach's sensitivity to fried foods.

I squeezed myself in the train's toilet closet—all stainless steel and mirrors, which were dull from years of use—and made do.

A lot of it, actually.

"Splattered" perhaps best described the explosive effect of Maastricht's codfish fillets.

Anyway, I finished about the time the train pulled away from the station, but, to my dismay, the toilet wouldn't flush. No matter how often I pressed the 'flush' button, my deposit remained in the basin.

The stench permeated the cramped space, so I quickly washed up and exited the toilet, offering a sheepish grin to the gentleman waiting for his turn.

Our train returned late to Eindhoven, which afforded me little time to pack and turn in at a reasonable hour, knowing I must get up early the following morning to catch an early train to Antwerp in order to meet Ann the Local for a ride to Brussels.

I relaxed in bed on the penultimate night of my trip, tantalizingly close to returning to America, seeing my family again, and being back where I belong.

*The author posing on the Saint Servatius Bridge,
a scenic overpass spanning the Meuse River in Maastricht.*

*The scenic Vrijthof in central Maastricht offers
an abundance of inviting restaurants.*

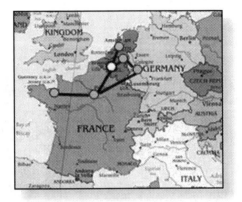

CHAPTER 6

Beautiful Belgium

Beginning the day with a pre-dawn alarm jolting me from the depths of a dreamy rest immediately put me in a bad mood. I'm usually a heavy sleeper and can't be shocked awake with a strategically-placed cattle prod, but it would be my destiny on my final morning in Europe to awake suddenly and displeased.

Irritated with the early hour (6:00 a.m.) and stressed from time constraints, I practically opened the morning buffet, scarfing down a meager breakfast as my appetite hadn't yet caught up with my semi-alertness. Not even having the first selections at the plentiful breakfast buffet—I highly recommend the powdered sugar chocolate croissants and fried squid rings, by the way—could elevate my disposition to a more pleasant level.

Gopal and I made our train with a few minutes to spare (when I return to Europe, you can bet your first born child that I won't race around trying to catch trains like I have on this trip; it's too nerve-racking). Our destination: Antwerp, Belgium, by way of connections in small towns named Breda and Roosendaal.

Antwerp is a large city—about half a million within the city limits and whose metropolitan area well exceeds a million—located in northern Belgium near the Netherlands border. It's on the right bank of the river Scheldt, linked to the North Sea by the Westerschelde.

We arrived at Antwerp Central Station—a beautiful building dating to the early 1900s with two massive neo-baroque façades, a large metal and glass dome, and a gilt and marble interior—with an hour to spare before meeting Ann the Local, who would drive us to Brussels. Instead of sitting in the station, Gopal suggested we head into Antwerp to see as many sites as possible until the time came to hop back on the train (we had to ride one station further to reach the rendezvous point).

It took us a few minutes to secure a city map, navigate the station's crooked corridors (many train stations are aged and have steps where escalators should be; not good for those toting swollen, weighty suitcases), and purchase tram tickets. We must have wasted 20 minutes, and when we boarded a crammed underground tram for a brief five-minute ride to the Groenplaats station—an elderly woman sat at my knee, fingers plugged firmly in each ear to guard against the screeching tram as it navigated sharp turns—we had maybe twenty minutes of sightseeing at our disposal.

It's difficult to see the sights in a 'hit and run' approach, especially with luggage and briefcase in tow, but we made the best of it.

We ascended to street level via an escalator to the tolling of cathedral bells echoing through the Groenplaats plaza. To our right, the Cathedral of Our Lady, Antwerp dominated the view.

Started in 1351 and finished in 1518, the Gothic cathedral is the tallest structure in Antwerp (its spire is 123 meters high—a little more than 400 feet). We were unable to enter—not that we could have for we had no time—because a funeral was in progress; we arrived just in time to see a coffin removed from the rear of a long black hearse, surrounded by a minor crowd, television cameras filming every move. It struck me that the cathedral bells tolled not for the hour but in reverence of the memorial service.

A block further, we came upon the Antwerp City Hall, or Stadhuis, on the western edge of Antwerp's Grote Markt (Great Market Square), where vendors delivered food and drinks to restauranteurs, who busied themselves sweeping sidewalks and cleaning tabletops. Erected in the 1560s, the impressive City Hall was festooned with colorful national flags flying from each of its three floors, and a statue in the middle of the square spewed streams of water, which fell on stacked boulders at its base.

We snapped a few photos then rushed a block further to the bank of the river Scheldt, where an elevated portico offered picturesque vistas, including Het Steen (literally 'The Stone'), a restored riverfront fort with large turrets, the last remaining remnant of 19th Century Antwerp fortifications.

The end of our allotted time upon us, I swiftly strode back to the subway, the jackhammer-like effect of dragging a 50-lb. suitcase over cobblestone paths tiring my arms and chafing my palms.

Ann the Local had waited only a few minutes past the prearranged time, and she drove us to Brussels, a half-hour away.

After checking into our hotel and grabbing a take-out sandwich from the same subway vendor that prompted our desperate search for an ATM the prior week, I ate in the office break room before afternoon meetings with the Brussels marketing team.

The end of the day came swiftly, and when Gopal and some of the Brussels staff left for happy hour at a nearby bar, I politely declined. No disrespect to present company, but I needed to separate myself from the work and the people, desiring to spend the balance of my last evening in Europe in my own company, strolling around the majestic Grand Place at my leisure, selecting a restaurant with only my tastes in mind, skirting the conversational demands of a group dinner. I am a man comfortable in my own skin, and, while it may seem antisocial, there are times that I need a break from others, to lose myself in my own thoughts, to savor glorious silence, and this was one of those times.

I went directly from work to the Galleries Royales St. Hubert—the covered plaza near our hotel—and bought Belgian chocolates for Lana and the boys at the Newhaus shop. I took them back to my room and, my appetite not yet whetted, remained in the hotel bar, where I knocked back a couple of Stella Artois beers while reading a book I brought from home. I lingered for over an hour at a street-facing table for three, legs propped up on the opposite chair, drinking and reading, though probably a little too much of the former as two beers on an empty stomach made my head swim and, as I left on a quest for dinner, my legs a bit unsteady.

I circumvented the Grand Place and its Friday night crowds, wobbling instead through narrow alleys on its periphery, falling behind two English-speaking gents because (1) they seemed to comprehend the French menus posted on restaurant windows, and (2) it kept me focused on dinner thereby distracting me from my Belgian beer buzz.

Selecting a restaurant from the countless options overloaded my remaining brain cells, further muddling my thoughts. Everything appeared so tasty and tempting, at least on paper, but nothing spoke to me. I wandered for over 30 minutes, studying menus, looking over shoulders to see what people were eating (many of them ate mussels in steaming black pots the size of small beach pails. Mussels are a delicacy in Europe but I don't like them enough to consume two dozen at a sitting).

On the Rue Grétry, I happened upon a quaint Italian bistro, intriguingly named "La Corte Gastronomica." I chose it because not only would it satisfy my hankering for pasta, it seemed agreeable to my digestive system.

The waiter placed me at a sidewalk table and I ordered a liter of water (to clear my head) and meat-filled tortellini in a rich cream sauce (to clear my bottom), which I consumed one delicious tortellini at a time, savoring every bite, sopping fresh French bread in the velvety sauce, gazing at the sidewalk activity, engrossed in the moment.

At the end of the meal, I lingered at the table, reading a book to let my food settle as I didn't want to be early for my date with a chocolate waffle. It struck me that if I tried reading after dinner in an American restaurant, the staff would likely pull my chair out from under me and sweep me out the door faster than you can say, "Table for two." But such is the case in Europe that the issue is moot, and I loitered for an additional twenty minutes before departing.

'La Chaloupe d'Or' is the name of the eatery on the Grand Place opposite City Hall where my chocolate waffle 'cherry' had been busted the week before. So it was without hesitation that I strode confidently to a sidewalk patio and ordered a chocolate waffle posthaste.

The Grand Place is an amazing sight, and, following dessert, a pang of disappointment gnawed at me as I stood in the middle of the plaza, soaking in for the last time the backlit Gothic spires and gilded houses before I strolled soberly to the hotel and turned in for the evening.

On the left is the colorful City Hall on the western edge of Antwerp's Grote Markt (Great Market Square).

Het Steen (literally 'The Stone') is a restored riverfront fort and the last remaining remnant of 19th Century Antwerp fortifications.

CHAPTER 7

Miscellaneous Observations

Over the course of my travels, I noted a number of miscellaneous observations—random thoughts, if you will—due mainly to my curious eye for detail. These observations I noted on a small pad kept in my back pocket throughout the trip; my colleagues often teased me when I retrieved it to make notes ("Uh oh. Jeff's going to write something down!")

* When Europeans go on vacation, they are "on holiday".
* Written dates in Europe place the day before the month and year, which is to say that 12 / 9 isn't the 9th of December but the 12th of September.
* Water in European restaurants isn't often free. Because many Europeans drink bottled water, you order it the same as you'd order a Coke or a glass of wine. And you have to specify whether you want it 'sparkling' or 'natural' (also called 'still'). I learned this quickly as sparkling water tasted like Sprite without the sugar water and left an aftertaste that lingered for hours (not to mention it made me burp like a baby).

* Europeans keep time 'military-style', so unless you're used to reading, say, 6:15 p.m. as 18:15 then you'll forever adjust the time in your head.
* Europe is extraordinarily conscious of the environment. No lights unnecessarily left on. Everyone recycles. One hotel no longer offered bars of soap and shampoo, favoring instead refillable soap/shampoo dispensers mounted on the shower walls.
* Want to use a public restroom in Europe? You better keep spare change in your pocket. Public restrooms are limited in number and those you find often have attendants, whose primary job is to keep the restrooms clean. It's customary to pay, say, 25 Euro cents to 1€, though the exact amount is always posted, either on a sign by the door or, in some cases, on a turnstile guarding access to the toilet.
* Drinks in restaurants are served without ice unless specifically requested. Not just alcoholic drinks, but water and soda as well. I don't know if it's cultural, but it is commonplace nonetheless.
* Diet Coke in Europe is called 'Coke Light' (not 'lite', which is a beer term). The word 'diet' is omitted for legal reasons.
* Europeans love their dogs. They take them everywhere! It's a practice allowed virtually everywhere—stores, restaurants, and hotels, to name a few—and these are the best behaving dogs I'd ever seen. They rested quietly and contentedly at their owner's feet, panting away as their masters ate, drank, and chatted away the hours. It wasn't until we were in the Antwerp Central Station on the final day of the trip that I first heard a dog bark. Amazing!
* Europeans use a comma rather than a decimal point to divide Euro dollars and Euro cents. For example, Americans write ten dollars and fifty cents as $10.50 but Europeans write the same amount as 10,50€.
* Europeans differ from Americans in the way they use their knife and fork while dining. After cutting a portion of food, Americans usually put down the knife before scooping up or stabbing the food with the fork. Europeans, on the other hand, use their knife to drag the food on top of the fork before lifting it to their mouths.

* If served bread in a restaurant, Europeans break off a bite then butter it, as opposed to Americans, who often butter the entire roll. Come to think of it, I believe the European way is proper etiquette, but who's counting?

* Order coffee in Europe and you're likely to have it served in a cup roughly the size of two shot glasses, which contradicted the 'Big Gulp' mentality of Americans, who must drink massive quantities from monster thermoses.

* European hotel beds are often covered with a duvet, a type of bedding common in northern Europe, a soft, flat bag traditionally filled with down or feathers and used on a bed as a blanket. Upon further research, I learned that duvets reduce the complexity of making a bed, as it is a single cover instead of the combination of two sheets, blankets, and quilts or other bed covers, traditional in many parts of the world. Sleeping under a duvet took a *whole lot* of getting used to, as I often sleep under a thin sheet, but a duvet weighs on you like three quilts.

* Computer keyboards in France are very different than those in the West, with letters located in different places, only one shift key (bottom right), characters I've never seen before, and numbers that require pressing the shift key. Before I realized the keyboard differences on the PC in my Paris hotel's business center, I'd been typing away for five minutes, and one glance at the monitor revealed a paragraph of gibberish as though typed by a child. It's just another way for the French to be different, I guess.

* A piece of travel advice: if you ever take a two week trip—it doesn't have to be to Europe; it could be anywhere—include fingernail clippers in your hygiene bag. My nails are getting so long that if I don't cut them soon I'm going to need a manicure.

* And perhaps the biggest observation I've made: Europe is absolutely steeped in history. If not for natural formations like the Grand Canyon, historical sites in America are aged but a fraction of their European counterparts, which makes sense given America's limited history, but, frankly, Americans' world perceptions have become obscured by a my-country-is-best

mentality. 'Historical' in America is—what? A town square? A Civil War battlefield? Independence Hall? Or maybe a teepee or Indian burial mound? America can't hold a historical candle to Europe, and I'm extremely thankful for the opportunity to have experienced another perspective of the world, with cultures and countries far more historically diverse than mine, where time recorded events long before America was a glint in somebody's eye.

Final thoughts: I loved the country charm of the Netherlands, the big city charisma of Brussels, the food and sights of Paris, the sincerity of the Germans. It was most definitely a trip to remember, and I hope to return again soon, next time with Lana in tow. I can't imagine a more memorable holiday than to return to these beautiful countries, my best friend at my side.

It's 4:37 a.m. Sunday morning. Sitting at my kitchen table, unable to sleep due to jet lag, I savored the glorious silence of the pre-dawn inky black stillness. A few minutes earlier, I tiptoed up the stairs to spy on the boys, slowly pushing open their door, finding my oldest son, Will, asleep on the floor in between the beds and his younger brother, Jack, lying diagonal across his, mostly exposed from the covers. I placed a tender kiss on their backs and slipped from their room, pulling the door closed behind me, knowing that in a few hours the day would start anew with fresh expectations, a new opportunity to experience the world, whether in Collierville, Bells or Brussels, a beacon always shining, guiding us to where we belong.

Home!

APPENDIX

Halfway Around the World: India

Day 1—Departure

Greetings from India!

Good morning, everyone! Well, it's morning *here* anyway. VERY early morning. I'm in a hotel halfway around the world, wide awake despite the early hour, feeling sleepy but otherwise fine.

I still can't believe that I'm actually here. Putting aside my inability to sleep, it's hard for my mind to get around the notion that I'm literally on the other side of the world. In my world, being on 'the other side of the world' usually means that Lana's trying to tell me something and my mind is a thousand miles away, in which case I might wish I was on the other side of the world.

But in this case, I'm really there.

So you might be asking, "Why am I in India?" For work, of course. Most of you probably know my frugal tendencies preclude spending thousands of dollars for round-trip business fare to Asia just for the fun of it. So, I'm here on official company business; more specifically, an in-depth study of India's transportation industry, with specific focus on how our competitors operate in this fast-growing market.

And is it fast-growing!

India and China are the two most populous countries in the world, and each is an emerging market with high growth rates. FedEx has a presence in both countries, but so does our competitors.

My group has been tasked by FedEx senior management to analyze the Indian transportation market and report back with recommendations for future business opportunities. There's only so much research we can do via the Internet and secondary sources, so our European counterparts suggested a trip to India to fill in the informational gaps.

I'm accompanied by a co-worker, who's chairing the team driving this analysis (I'm the co-chair). His name is Gopalakrishnan, but we call him Gopal (sounds like go-PALL). He's a native of India, which, frankly, takes a load off my mind. Being the anti-adventurous type, I can't imagine coming to India by myself. I'd be a nervous wreck, navigating a foreign culture, knowing no one, thousands of miles from home and family (not to mention home cooking).

It's a very sobering thought being so far from home. But now you can imagine what it must have been like for Gopal to come to America.

I have so much respect for those who have the courage—and it takes a LOT of courage—to leave the comfort zone of home and move to another culture. I understand why they did it, but I don't think I'm strong enough to do it myself. Maybe I'm too much of a momma's boy who'd rather be close to my family. If I want to go home, all I have to do is pack up the minivan and drive an hour or two, maybe spending $50 to fill up the gas tank. If Gopal wants to go home, it requires thousands of dollars and a day and a half of international travel. It's mentally, physically, financially and emotionally challenging.

Gopal is tall (6'4") and lean with distinctive Indian features—jet black hair, Coppertone skin, dark eyes—and a disarming smile. He's also a newlywed. His wife, Vidya, is a consultant who spends most of the workweek in St. Louis, so they're apart a lot. They take turns driving back and forth to see each other on weekends.

Today, she drove him to the airport to see him off. It was a sweet scene, the two of them saying goodbye. I could sense that perhaps she felt somewhat envious that Gopal was going home—albeit on business—while she remained in Memphis.

I was surprised how much preparation is necessary to visit a foreign land. For example, I learned that immunizations were required for travel to India. Lots of them, actually, due primarily to water-borne diseases which Americans rarely think about.

I called the local health department to ask what shots were required. They said I needed shots for hepatitis A (two shots given six months apart), hepatitis B (three shots given four months apart), typhoid, and tetanus (which I needed anyway because ten years had passed since I accidentally stabbed myself in the palm while slicing a frozen bagel with the sharpest knife in the kitchen. Not my brightest decision.) I have no fear of needles (except perhaps the épée anesthesiologists use to administer epidurals. When my wife gave birth to our first child, I got down on my knees and thanked God I have a penis), but, boy, was my arm sore!

Additionally, passports alone won't gain travelers entry into India. Americans must obtain a visa from an Indian embassy before being allowed into the country. I presumed they wanted to confirm I wasn't a child-molesting ax murderer or desired to import Britney Spears music to Bollywood. Anyway, visas are mostly a formality, unless, in my case, one had only a week to put travel affairs in order, in which case completing the process by snail mail would've required a presidential decree.

So, a few days before my departure, my employer flew me to Washington, D.C., where I applied for the visa in person at the Indian embassy. I arrived a day early and spent the evening at my brother's home. I awoke the next day at a reasonable—read, late-hour and casually rode the subway into the city, leisurely walking from the train station to the Indian embassy, located on Massachusetts Avenue N.W., a scenic tree-lined road known as "Embassy Row", which was once the premier residential neighborhood housing Washington's elite in spacious mansions, but now housed worldwide embassies and diplomatic institutions.

I dropped off my paperwork and was told I could pick it up at the end of the day, which, thankfully, meant I could forego waiting for hours in a crowded room that smelled of curry. I spent a relaxed day in D.C., visiting museums, lunching with a old college friend, stopping in a Barnes & Noble and happening upon a bustling book signing by former American Idol-winner Fantasia (How can a girl who supposedly can't read write a book, anyway?)

All told, it was a pleasant way to spend a "working" day. I was so relaxed that I patiently tolerated the moderate wait to retrieve my visa. My return flight home wasn't until the next morning anyway, and I eagerly anticipated a tasty dinner cooked by Chuck, my brother's jovial father-in-law.

By the time I returned to my brother's home, the aroma of grilled hamburgers permeated the air. I grabbed a cold beer from the fridge and joined Chuck on the back deck.

"What's that smell?" he muttered, sniffing the air in my vicinity as I saddled up to the grill.

I shrugged my shoulders, taking a long drag from the beer bottle.

"Hmmm," he added, with furrowed brow. "Smells like curry."

My emotions ran the gamut from giddy excitement to paralyzing fear. My international travels had been limited to a week-long Caribbean cruise with my parents and grandparents ("Limbo, anyone?"), a "cup of coffee" 36-hour business trip to Peru (which, technically, is an overseas trip, but flying over the Gulf of Mexico and calling it "overseas" is like children banging on a piano and calling it "music"), and a high school Spanish Club trip to Mexico, where I consumed my first alcoholic drink, an unfriendly Glen Livet and water, my father's favorite drink and the only option that sprang to my muddled mind clouded by peer pressure and inexperience. It was unquestionably the vilest liquid I've ever consumed.

Frankly, my exposure to foreign cultures had been limited to cross-border trips into Mississippi. So the anxiety preceding my first "real" international trip far exceeded the excitement of experiencing another culture.

We left Memphis early Saturday afternoon and flew a puddle jumper to Chicago, where we grabbed a bite to eat during a three hour layover. We spent most of the time in the Swiss Air business class lounge.

But once I boarded the intercontinental plane, I acted like the proverbial kid in the candy store.

One professional benefit I have in working for a Fortune 500 company with a billion-dollar travel & entertainment budget is that even low-level peons may fly business class on international trips, given the great distance. I've lobbied the company's Global Travel department that flights from Tennessee to Florida are technically 'international' on account of the vast social and cultural differences, but they stopped returning my calls years ago.

Anyway, international business class travel is, using a popular term, "da bomb", especially on a foreign airline. Comparing international carriers' service to that in the U.S. is like comparing Da Vinci to a pre-school finger painter.

For example, when my colleague and I boarded a Swiss Air flight for the first leg of our nearly-around-the-world journey, I found it refreshing when a perky flight attendant pointed us in the direction of our seats, where a personal pillow and blanket awaited us. Resting atop the pillow were a set of headphones and a "refreshing tissue" tightly sealed in a small packet and sponsored by one of my company's chief rivals. I figured I'd save it to refresh my anus after the bowel movement that would surely follow the consumption of whatever food they planned to serve.

Another item awaiting us was a black faux leather pouch secured by red laces—I think "amenity kit" is the technical term for it but to me it was no less than a goody bag. It contained mainly hygiene items—ear plugs (to block out the noisy kids in working class), black socks (long enough that if I stuck my feet in them I could pull them up to my thighs), and eye shades, to name a few.

In the first ten minutes after being seated, I merrily tore open the many giveaways, babbling juvenile comments like, "Hey! Look! A fold-up toothbrush!"

Business class seats weren't the hip-pinching, knee-busting, muscle-cramping torture chairs found in coach. No, these were spacious and, dare I say, comfortable. I could extend my legs, *and my feet wouldn't touch the seat in front of me!* I demonstrated this to my colleague—emphasizing my glee with a goofy smile—but, he being the taller of the two, couldn't do the same.

"Oh, well," he lamented. "Nothing's built for me."

Business class seats are also multimedia centers. Embedded in the armrest on my left was a futuristic-looking remote that controlled the functions on my personal TV screen, a roughly 12" monitor which folded inside a panel under the left armrest and could be retrieved by lifting the pad.

Embedded in my right armrest adjacent to my thigh were the seat controls. And I'm not talking about the ubiquitous gray button that reclines the seat all of three inches. There were five settings: two for the footrest (which extended much like a recliner), two for the lumbar settings, and the last for the back, which reclined to a comfortable but not quite horizontal setting. There was even a headrest which could be adjusted for one's comfort. My colleague showed me how to tug on its ends and what at first looked flat could be molded into a U-shaped support that would keep your head from flopping from side to side, which I hoped he appreciated because I tend to drool when I sleep.

It wasn't long after I grew accustomed to my modified La-Z-Boy when a stewardess—flight attendant, whatever—presented a tray with an assortment of drinks that looked like water, orange juice, and wine. I chose the latter, desiring alcoholic buzz over hydration (not always the best choice when traveling by air, so I'm told). Besides, who was I to pass up a complimentary glass of wine? My colleague—a tall vegetarian, non-alcohol-drinking Indian national named Gopal, more on him later—chose water. We clinked our glasses together and toasted our good fortune to be sitting in the forward section, though I almost choked on my drink after the first sip; the bubbly carbonation fizzing my nasal cavities revealing my selection of not wine but champagne.

All the better, I thought, wiping the excess from my chin.

I turned my attention to the multimedia options at my disposal. A few clicks on my handy-dandy remote took me to a screen that presented a multitude of choices, including video (24 movie choices), audio (16 music channels, including Arabic music, which isn't bad actually), games (ten choices, including 'Who Wants to Be A Millionaire?', Pong, and Swiss Ski Challenge, to name a few), and shopping (which was currently unavailable—darn luck that!).

Television monitors hanging on the bulkhead above the center section offered the requisite welcomes in five languages (English, German, French, Italian, and a language I'd never heard of—and didn't retain, even after asking—which the stewardess, er, flight attendant said was a language spoken by a small fraction (50,000 people according to her) of the Swiss population), interspersed with rotating views offering flight operation minutiae.

In the first view, a diminutive white Swiss Air plane crept slowly across a world map along a dotted line, which represented our flight path, and pinpointed with GPS-precision our actual position. The map then morphed into screens displaying miscellaneous flight statistics, like distance to destination, ground speed, altitude above sea level, and time to destination, continuously updated in real time as we ascended.

I'd glance up and notice our ground speed at 530 mph. A moment later, it refreshed to 562. Then 617. 647. And so on. I'd turn away and, upon turning back, spot the same data converted to metric measurements. Then the English descriptions became French then German.

Gopal thought it best to complete some work before dinner. I emphasize that *he* thought it best because I wanted to work about as much as Kim Kardashian wants a long-term relationship. Nevertheless, I attempted—albeit half-heartedly—to immerse myself in dry business reading, but I was far too wired to maintain the attention span required to retain anything, what with the lure of movies, music and more at my fingertips.

Roughly half an hour after take-off, the flight attendants distributed dinner menus throughout the cabin. These were classy menus: multi-colored, multi-language, glossy tri-fold brochures, with a multitude of options, none of them the 'snack pack' of Oreos, processed cheese sticks, and beef jerky. The North America to Switzerland dinner included two courses, a selection of cheeses, and dessert, presented in three languages.

The first course offered a choice of gravlax and grilled shrimp served with white radish and hot honey mustard, or seasonal salad with a balsamic and olive oil dressing. I ate the former, though not without some hesitancy ('gravlax' evoked images of something used to patch asphalt roads), and found it mild and tasty (I would learn later that gravlax is a Scandinavian dish, usually served as an appetizer, and consisted of salmon cured in salt, sugar, and dill).

The main course offered four choices: beef tenderloin in a brandy and peppercorn sauce served with spinach, fennel and roasted potato; veal sausage accompanied by green beans, rosti and an onion sauce (this being the 'taste of Switzerland' option); sea bass with ginger and soy served with bok choy, carrots and miso sauce (the low carb option), and roasted eggplant and spinach lasagna in a tomato sauce with ricotta, mozzarella and parmesan cheese (the no-way-I'm-gonna-eat-this-shit vegetarian option).

I chose the tenderloin. Gopal chose the eggplant.

Dessert featured chocolate delight with raspberry sauce, a kind of mousse concoction, though a bit too heavy on the sauce. In typical chocoholic fashion, I ate it up, careful not to consume the portion touching the raspberry sauce. The stewardess—I mean, flight attendant—brought Gopal a fruit bowl, but he longed for a chocolate dessert. He asked for one, but the last one remaining could only be found on her dinner tray, which, to my surprise, she gladly offered (this may reflect poorly on me, but the only way I would've given up my chocolate dessert is for someone to pry it from my cold, dead hands). Ever the gentleman, Gopal refused to take her dessert, but she insisted and he accepted it gracefully.

According to GPS TV, we ate dinner over Quebec and dessert over Nova Scotia, still only a fraction through our 4,435 mile journey that would span seven time zones. I found particularly interesting a view showing a flat map of the world, half of it shaded, which reflected areas at night. Our GPS-tracked plane crept slowly east while the shaded area of night crept slowly west.

I settled into my chair, reclined to a comfortable position, extended my footrest, kicked back, and relaxed for a while.

It was soon thereafter a steward—or whatever they call male flight attendants these days—walked to our row with a box of Swiss chocolates, asking if we would like any. In his thick accent, it came out something like, "Vould you like someving from za choc'lates box?"

I chuckled and shot Gopal my best Cheshire grin that screamed, in true Tweety Bird fashion, "He don't know me vewy well, do he?"

Only half-jokingly, I asked if I could have the whole box.

He allowed me to select two pieces, which immediately and deliciously melted in my mouth.

"I have to buy some of these when we get to Zurich," I told Gopal. I knew I'd have to buy two boxes because one of them would never make it home.

The adrenaline which had fueled my initial excitement soon wore off. My head began to throb in that annoying, sinus pressure way, and my contact lenses suddenly felt dry and uncomfortable. I often slept poorly on airplanes, but I nevertheless attempted to rest. I kicked back again and closed my eyes, but napped fitfully, at best.

When the cabin lights blinked on a few hours later, I slowly recovered my bearings, noticing on the operations screen that we had skirted the southern tip of the UK and were crossing the English Channel into northern France. The cabin crew rolled out carts to serve breakfast (fresh fruits, yogurt, breakfast breads, coffee and tea).

A short-while later, I opened my window shade to witness the sun peeking over the horizon, illuminating the snow-capped peaks of the Alps rising above cloud-covered valleys that resembled a sea of undulating cotton.

Gopal said our descent into Zurich should be scenic but the dense fog precluded any scenic Swiss vistas. Visibility shrank to zero as we descended through opaque clouds.

Gopal and I were discussing how to ration time during our 90-minute layover when suddenly the plane shook with a terrifying, violent thud. I thought it would be just my luck for my first overseas trip to be marred by an airline calamity, leaving my wife and kids without a husband and father.

I have a very active imagination, which is good for writing fiction and entertaining Cub Scouts, but a hindrance when hot button stress points are aggravated by the slightest bit of anxiety.

I remember once boarding a plane, just ahead of a gentleman who would be my seatmate on a later international flight. As I sat down, he approached on my periphery. He handed his coat to a flight attendant while I fussed about my seat, frowning, unable to locate the amenity kit which was supposed to be there.

It took a moment before I realized he was talking to me.

"Excuse me?"

"Dis is an old plane, no?"

He was a pleasant-looking chap—medium height, kind smile, thinning brown hair dusted by wisps of gray. He spoke with a distinctive accent, probably Dutch, given our destination of Amsterdam. He reached in a pocket and retrieved a Blackberry, which he placed on the console between our seats before lowering himself with a loud exhale.

His question took me completely by surprise. I'm not often asked to evaluate the age of an aircraft that would soon propel me 4,500 miles at 600 miles an hour, 31,000 feet above an ice-cold ocean. Frankly,

I'd rather not dwell on gruesome possibilities like, say, stripped rivets suddenly working themselves out of the fuselage somewhere over the North Atlantic.

Besides, who talks like that to complete strangers anyway? In this age of heightened security and testy nerves, it should be a crime to put ominous thoughts in the minds of air travelers.

My mother always said, 'If you can't say something nice to somebody, don't say anything at all." Okay, well, she actually said, "If you can't say something nice *about* somebody . . ." but the point still stands, though I suspected my seatmate probably talked like that *about* other people, too. ("See that flight attendant? She is an old hag, no?").

Anyhow, it's sometimes difficult to suppress fatalist thoughts. My father's untimely death at age 47 precluded him from watching his sons marry and spoiling his grandchildren, so perhaps my irrational fears are the result of being a concerned dad and husband who wants to remain on Earth as long as possible.

Either that or I watched too many "Faces of Death" videos as a teenager.

"You think so?" I replied, trying to appear undisturbed.

"Yah," he exclaimed, looking around, appraising the environment. "Dis is *definitely* an old plane."

(I would learn later that it really *was* and old plane: a DC-10, probably dating to the Disco Era).

So, why wasn't the crew showing any sign of alarm when we'd clearly hit something on our approach? Was I the only one panicking?

Yes, I was.

That "something" turned out to be the runway.

You can imagine my surprise—and embarrassment—that it was a simple matter of the cloud cover being so thick at such a low altitude that I couldn't see the ground until we landed. It took a few minutes before my pulse returned to a normal rhythm.

After I got over my "plane age" anxieties, I asked 5B if we were supposed to get an amenity kit.

"Yah," he answered, nodding. "Dey'll bring it soon."

"Oh, good," I said, explaining how easily pleased I can be, wanting the kit, that is.

He chuckled.

"You must be easily pleased or you don't travel very much."

"Both, actually," I answered, smiling.

He gave me his amenity kit when we arrived at our destination.

The third segment involved another 8-9 hour flight from Zurich to Mumbai. Because I rested little on the Zurich flight, I committed myself to getting some sleep on the Mumbai flight.

It's these moments that screamed for drugs. In my case, a couple of Ambien pills—free samples from my primary care physician—did the trick. Shortly after our second flight departed Zurich, I popped two pills and I slept through two meals, and half of the movie *War of the Worlds* (which, in hindsight, would've been a natural sleeping pill).

I awoke maybe halfway into the flight, somewhere over the Middle East. I'd slept through lunch, which was fine because I needed the sleep more than another multi-course meal. While Gopal slept across the aisle from me, I jotted down a few notes in my journal.

We landed at the Mumbai Airport about 10:30 p.m. local time, an hour later than scheduled because the runway for wide-body aircraft had been shut down because another plane had overshot the runway and the airport wasn't letting anyone else land until they cleared the plane. We thought we might be diverted to the Ahmadabad Airport an hour away, which would have really thrown a kink into our already tight schedule due to a national holiday later in the week when everything would be shut down, which gave us only four days to complete our work. We couldn't afford to lose another day, but things worked out because we landed on a shorter runway, using every bit of it. After we landed, the pilot made a u-turn and high-tailed it off the runway to clear it for the next arrival. Some passengers clapped their approval once safely at the terminal.

Clearing customs took remarkably little time. The queues were short, they stamped my visa in maybe a minute, my bag was waiting for me at baggage claim, and we passed through exit security in relative ease. A hotel car awaited us and we arrived at our hotel around 11:00 p.m.

After checking in, I called home and talked to Lana and the boys for a while, but it was getting close to midnight and I wanted to hang up my clothes and hit the sack.

I woke up at 3:00 a.m. after sleeping only two hours, exhausted but unable to sleep. Perhaps I should've taken another sleeping pill before going to bed.

Anyway, after nearly 9,000 miles and a dozen time zones, I'm on the other side of the world, sitting at a desk in my hotel room, watching a U.S. golf tournament on ESPN India (where the commercials promote cricket and soccer). Surreal as it seems, it's good to be here, though I miss everyone terribly. I have a lot of work to do and I'm sure the week will pass quickly. But, all things considered, there's no place like home.

Day 2—The First Day in Mumbai

I never did fall back asleep, but not for a lack of trying. I lay in bed for the longest time but knew I just wasn't going to sleep anymore. So I got out of bed about 5:45 a.m., laced up my running shoes, and waited for the fitness center to open at 6:00.

I ran three miles on the treadmill. At least, I think I did because all measurements are in metric. The scales in the fitness center are in kilograms. The treadmill settings are in kilometers. They drive on the wrong side of the road (which, granted, has nothing to do with metric measurements, but it's another unfamiliar aspect I'm dealing with). The guy next to me watched CNN and I saw that today's temperature is supposed to be 34.

That would be degrees Celsius, which I think is about 100 degrees. And it's a hot 100, too. Not a dry heat, but a heavy, muggy, overpowering heat that weighs on you like a damp quilt.

The fitness center is large and modern. Most cardio equipment has a personal video screen which can be tuned to a plethora of channels. I tuned mine to the Angels-Yankees ALCS game, which felt odd to watch a night baseball game while at the same time jogging to a vista of the morning sun rising over metropolitan Mumbai.

The service here is extraordinary (Gopal described it as "staggering"). The staff is exceedingly friendly. The rooms are spacious and clean. When I returned to the hotel in the evening, even the dirty clothes I had tossed in a nearby chair had been folded and neatly stacked.

There are room features I've never seen before. First, the key card that opens the door isn't inserted into a slot to open the door. Instead, one must push a button above the door handle and hold the card over the button, which scans the card and unlocks the door. Once inside, you insert the key card into a slot on the wall at eye level. This turns on the TV and most of the room lights. To turn everything off, simply remove the card from the wall.

The bathrooms are interesting, too. The tub and shower are sunken, which is to say you must descend stairs from floor level to use them. There is no shower door or shower curtain. Naturally, one must exercise caution when exiting the shower because the floors are marble and very slippery when wet.

Continuing with the bathroom design, the vanities are made of glass. And so is the sink. When I stand before the vanity, it's hard to see the concavity of the sink unless water droplets mark the contours. It looks like a flat sheet of glass until you get up close to it.

After showering following my workout, I stopped by Gopal's room, where I found him eating breakfast and watching the same baseball game (he's rooting very hard against the Yankees). I asked him what smelled so good and he offered me a bite.

"What is it?" I asked, always hesitant to put any food in my mouth unless I know what it is first.

"You'll like it," he said. "Trust me."

Famous last words, I thought, but relented.

He tore off a piece of what looked like a small quesadilla, dipped it in a sauce, and fed it to me, which created an awkward moment—on my part anyway—but it passed.

"This is good," I said. "What is it?"

Gopal had to answer my question three times before I got it.

I had eaten masaladosa, which is like a crepe with a potato stuffing. It would be my first taste of local Indian cuisine, and not the last.

I ate breakfast in the hotel restaurant while Gopal finished getting ready. It was a nice buffet spread, but nothing like those in America. I made a point to try a few unfamiliar foods. Two things I liked were akuri, which is scrambled eggs with local Indian spices, and aloo paratha, which is whole wheat, stuffed Indian bread. I ate some familiar foods, like croissants, breakfast hams and cereal, though I didn't eat much of the latter because upon the first spoonful I realized I had poured no ordinary milk over my Snap, Crackle and Pop. I returned to the buffet and learned it was soy milk (Ugh!).

Our FedEx host met us at the hotel a short time thereafter and drove us through narrow, gridlocked streets to his office.

If there's one word that describes Mumbai, it would be "crowded." India is the world's second most populous country—behind only China—with over 1 billion people (the combined population of India and China constitutes about a third of the world's population). India has three times more people but only one-third the land mass of the U.S. Imagine fitting a billion people in a geographic area the size of, say, the Midwestern and Mountain states.

Mumbai is situated on the western coast of India on the Arabian Sea and has about 15 million people, enough to rank it in the world's top five most populous cities. It's predominantly Hindu, but 20% of the population—about 200 million people, or 2/3 the population of the U.S.—is Muslim, which makes it the world's second largest Muslim population behind only Indonesia.

As we waited for the hotel valet to retrieve our host's car, I was struck by an unpleasant odor in the air. It had been bothering me—conceptually, not physically—since we arrived, but only when I exited the hotel could I identify it in the morning light.

Smog.

Air quality here is poor, at best. The morning light illuminated what I couldn't see the night before, namely a layer of haze that hung over the city like a bad boss. Even locals who walk the streets carry a handkerchief to cover their nose and mouth. I immediately began to despair the thought of clogged sinuses so far from my neighborhood Walgreens. I don't feel quite normal, which could be the dust or the effects from only six hours of sleep the past two nights.

The traffic was horrendous! Mumbai drivers make New York cabbies resemble Miss Manners graduates. Even the State Department web site states, "Travel by road in India is dangerous."

Buses are patronized by hundreds of millions of Indians, but they're driven fast, recklessly, and without consideration for the rules of the road, which appeared to be few, if any. Accidents, I'm told, are quite common, and given India's inferior infrastructure, the situation has digressed into a mass of autos struggling to navigate crowded streets and poorly maintained roads, where it appears to be 'every man for himself.'

On Indian roads, the safest driving policy is to assume that other drivers won't respond to a traffic situation in the same way I would in the U.S. For example, buses and trucks often run red lights and merge directly into traffic at yield points. Cars, auto-rickshaws (small, three-wheeled taxis ubiquitous to this world region), bicycles and pedestrians behave only slightly more cautiously. I've learned that Indian drivers tend to look only ahead and often consider themselves responsible only for traffic in front of them, not behind or to the side. There is a constant flickering of high beam headlights and a continuous din of blaring car horns as drivers frequently use them to announce their presence.

Outside the major cities, main roads and other roads are equally congested and poorly maintained. Even main roads often have just two lanes, with poor visibility and inadequate signs and warning markers. On the few divided highways, one often meets local transportation going the wrong way (I've already experienced this several times. Additionally, my host's car has no seat belts in the rear seat and, being a nervous rear seat passenger with no seat belt, I've been acutely wary of the danger). I've found the roadways to be congested with overcrowded buses, scooters, pedestrians, camel carts, and free roaming livestock.

Speaking of livestock, cows are revered in this culture. As I understand it, many Hindu rituals involve milk and those who follow this religion consider cows sacred. If a driver hits a cow, the vehicle and its occupants are at risk of being attacked by passersby. I'm told that these attacks pose significant risk of injury or death to the vehicle's occupants, not to mention potential incineration of the car (I'm not making this up). So this has led the State Department to advise on its India travel information web site that, "It can thus be unsafe to remain at the scene of an accident of this nature, and drivers may instead wish to seek out the nearest police station."

I won't bore you with the details of work today, but suffice it to say that Gopal and I spent the day interviewing assorted members of the FedEx India sales and marketing team, broken mid-day by lunch at Pizza Hut (Gopal wants to ease my sensitive tummy's introduction to Indian cuisine), which has some strange things on its menu, but offered a pepperoni pizza, which tasted exactly like one I might order for take-out at home.

I'm feeling the effects of no sleep and plan to take a sleeping pill tonight, which is what I should've done last night. I'm determined to get to bed and rise at a reasonably normal hour, which is to say that if I sleep seven or eight hours, I'll be a happy camper.

Day 3—All Around the Town

Jet lag in the days before drugs must have been a bear. Were it not for sleeping pills, I would still suffer its effects. But, thankfully, I took one before bed last night and slept through the night for the first time in days.

Slept at last.

Slept at last.

Thank God Almighty.

I slept at last.

The morning started in a more normal fashion, waking at a reasonable hour, though the showers have been far from reasonable, thanks to a lack of hot water. Gopal doesn't have the same problem and he says I should call the front desk to lodge a complaint, but it's really not that big a deal. I'm used to taking cold baths after long training runs, so a cold shower isn't too foreign. Besides, it's a good way to clear away the proverbial cobwebs after a drug-induced slumber.

I can easily see how sleeping pills become addictive. I began to feel its effects after only 10 minutes. Often I go to bed and find it difficult to turn my mind off, in which case I usually just lay there and assure myself that this, too, shall pass. Now that I know how effective the pills can be, it's enticing to use them. I mentioned this to Gopal, but he warned me that my body might rely on them to fall asleep.

It's good to have friends who watch out for you.

I took a final pill last night and watched cricket on ESPN India for a few minutes until I felt tired. Cricket is *very* popular in India. Gopal's been tutoring me on its rules, and I've learned that it's remarkably similar to baseball, perhaps even the inspiration for it. Gopal told me that one of our founding fathers—John Adams—is reported to have said during preparations for the Declaration of Independence that if cricket clubs can have a president, why not a country?

The bowler in cricket is equivalent to the pitcher in baseball, but the bowler must throw the ball stiff-armed without bending his elbow. Baseball has a catcher; cricket has a wicket-keeper. Baseball has a strike zone; cricket has wickets, which resemble three 2x4's stuck inches apart in the ground. Both sports have runs, innings (baseball has nine innings and games last maybe three hours, while cricket test matches have two innings and games can last up to five days), and bats (though a cricket bat reminds me of the paddle Mr. Watlington used to whip me in fifth grade after I fought Johnny Lee on the playground).

There are interesting differences as well. For example, a baseball field is diamond shaped with an outfield; a cricket field is a 360 degree circle. Baseball has four bases, laid out in a diamond; cricket has two, situated at either end of a rectangle. The best baseball teams score an average of five runs a game; the best cricket teams score runs in the hundreds. A home run in baseball depends on the number of runners on base but can't exceed four runs; a home run is cricket is always worth six runs.

I'm fascinated by cricket, but don't plan to watch it when I return to the States. I miss Major League Baseball!

Our day's plans involved making customer sales calls. After eating another hearty breakfast at the hotel (today I tried poha—yellow rice flakes tempered with Indian spices—and aloo bhaji—potatoes cooked in Indian spices), we scheduled three customer visits over the course of the day.

And we traversed much of Mumbai in the process, taking away some interesting tidbits from my observations of this crowded city.

First, elevators—called 'lifts'—are not always safe. I rode several that were straight out of the 1950s. Claustrophobic boxes packed with as many people that could fit in ten square feet. One even posted a sign that read, "Persons using the lift do so at their own risk. Management."

Great, I thought. I come all this way and I'm going to die in a tragic elevator accident. I wanted to suggest the stairs next time but I sensed our host has an aversion to stairwells, preferring to take the lift three floors rather than hoof it three flights. Perhaps because he's a smoker. Or maybe he's inured to the risks of living in Mumbai, water-borne diseases and treacherous traffic notwithstanding.

Second, when you're the minority in a city of, say, 15 million people, it's like the circus came to town. Our second meeting was held somewhere deep in the heart of old Mumbai—although it seems like most of Mumbai is 'old'. We navigated narrow one lane streets lined with pedestrians and shops to reach the office, which looked straight out of the Roosevelt administration. We parked in an adjacent alley, shaded by old trees, and then the show started.

As we stood in the shade, enjoying a cool breeze blowing in from the street, I could see in my peripheral vision workers emerging from a nearby shop, apparently curious about the white guy in a suit. For the first time since I arrived, the realization that I'm 9,000 miles from home sunk in. I tried not to look at them, but could sense the many eyes focused on me. My heart raced a bit—okay, more than a bit—and my anxiety was palpable, so much that I had trouble focusing at the customer interview. Not that I was in any danger, but I was glad when we left.

Third, I saw a few things that are culturally accepted here which wouldn't be perceived so favorably in the States. For instance, it's common that friends walking together may have one arm draped around the other's shoulder. It's a sign of friendship and has nothing to do with sexual orientation. When I asked Gopal about it, he said something to the effect that considering the horrendous traffic, government corruption, and other major social and political concerns, gay issues rank pretty far down the list. So even if it were a sexual gesture, people probably wouldn't notice.

Except for the white guy from Tennessee.

Well, it's about 11:15 p.m. here and getting late. I'm in Gopal's room and he's channel-surfing. He's watching Toon Disney. Something called Jet-X. Now it's on 'Seinfeld', a show about nothing, which describes much of the TV programming, although I probably shouldn't be so harsh.

It might help if I spoke the language and could understand what people are saying.

Yada yada yada.

Day 4—A Day Off

This evening's report comes from the hotel bar. Gopal has traveled to the suburbs to visit an aunt, so I'm on my own, enjoying a Kingfisher beer (compliments of the bartender), a bowl of peanuts at my side, swaying to the soft sounds of jazz playing over the speakers, typing on my Dell laptop in the muted light of the second-floor bar overlooking the lobby.

Today is a festival holiday, so work has taken a back seat to pleasure, a welcome break to the many hours we've put in. Tomorrow promises to be a busy day, as we're flying to Delhi for more customer calls. We'll be up at 5:00 a.m. to make a 7:00 a.m. flight and will return late in the evening. It's been nice to have a mental and physical respite.

Today's festival is called Dusshera, one of India's most popular Indian festivals. There is great religious significance I don't understand, but Gopal says the festival is one of the most important of festivals in the Hindu calendar and is marked by the worship of good over evil. Most businesses are closed, though you wouldn't know it by the shops and restaurants that remained open, but I'm getting ahead of myself.

So after a dawdling breakfast (I didn't try anything new today, preferring to stick to a more traditional Western breakfast) and a few slow-paced hours of work, Gopal and I asked the concierge to secure a car and driver for the day. One must be careful in Mumbai not to use just any cab service, for there are less than scrupulous providers who will not only rip you off but put you in danger, which is why we leveraged the concierge to secure a car and negotiate the terms. The total cost to us was 1,500 Indian rupees each, or about US$33. Not bad when you spread that over the course of a day.

Being a festival holiday, traffic was lighter than usual, so we made excellent time from the hotel to downtown, where our first destination was the Colaba Causeway, located in the heart of south Mumbai.

Rows of shops lined both sides of the street. Colaba is the tourist hub which runs parallel to the Gateway of India. Sidewalk stalls sold fake jewelry, t-shirts, cheap leather goods and knick-knacks; Bohemian cafes and budget hotels also dot this area.

Gopal proved to be an excellent advisor, not just in terms of which shops to patronize but also in analyzing the quality and price of the merchandise. He questioned me about Lana's tastes and styles, making educated suggestions based on my answers. Being a guy, I'm probably not as well versed as I should be on my wife's tastes.

Our conversations went something like this:

"So, what does she like?" he asked.

"That's hard to say."

"It is?"

"Well, I don't pay much attention to these things."

"Did she tell you what she wanted?"

"Yeah."

"And that was . . . ?

I told him.

"Is that all?"

"No. She'd probably like something else, too."

"Let's see what we can find then."

So, we went to several shops. The salesperson would approach and Gopal totally took the lead, describing what we sought, evaluating the quality, alerting me to something that was overpriced, mostly speaking in English but occasionally speaking in Hindi. I found it fascinating to watch him work the vendors. He's very skilled.

I'm glad he's on my team.

We eventually found a place offering sufficient quality at a reasonable price. Then it was time for a quick lunch at McDonald's before traveling to Mumbai's most striking monument.

Situated on the southeast tip of Mumbai is the Gateway of India. Built in 1911 to commemorate the visit of King George V and Queen Mary to India, the monument is traditionally the first thing visitors arriving by boat would see of Mumbai, akin to the Statue of Liberty in New York.

We took a few photos and absorbed the scenery, but we didn't stay long. The crowds were thick on account of the holiday and the place is notorious for pickpockets, so we kept our hands in our pockets a lot.

From the Gateway our driver took us to the Hanging Gardens via Marine Drive, which fronts the bay and is also called the "Queen's Necklace" because of the dramatic curve of its streetlights at night. I'm told it's a striking sight in the evening from the higher elevations.

The Hanging Gardens date to 1881 when they were laid on a reservoir on the hills overlooking the bay. The terraced gardens provide sunset views over the Arabian Sea. There are incredible vistas there, but remain mostly blocked by tall trees. The park has such potential—much like Mumbai—but inertia and government indifference makes it an afterthought, so it remains an underutilized asset.

After visiting the Gardens we departed for the hotel, passing open parks filled with people relaxing and playing games of cricket, a Muslim mosque that dates back hundreds of years, and people dancing in the streets to the upbeat sounds of festival music, garlands of saffron flowers and mango leaves draped around their necks.

But that's not what struck me most.

Gopal and I were engrossed in conversation, discussing religion, as I recall, when we were interrupted by a tap on my window. I'd become used to peddlers approaching our car while we waited for traffic lights to change. A wave of the hand usually dismissed them with barely an afterthought.

But this wasn't a peddler.

I turned to find a woman standing on the other side of my door. She cradled a baby in her arms. Crying, she gestured to the child, and while I couldn't understand her words, I most definitely understood what she meant.

The baby was hungry.

I shook my head gently. The woman then leaned her head against my window and began to sob, the desperation painfully evident, a despondent mother's anguish laid bare for this foreigner's eyes to see, my heart breaking with every second.

She moved on to the car behind us, and I resisted the compulsion to turn around. I thought about how much I have—in her eyes, I'm probably rich beyond belief—but instead I did nothing, rationalizing my decision in the way many of us do: if I give to her, then what do I do for the next person? Where do I draw the line?

I've been thinking about them a lot, the image of a hungry baby burned into my memory. It's ironic that I was engrossed in a conversation about religion when our paths crossed because it could be argued that my inaction was decidedly sacreligious.

The poverty in Mumbai is extensive and pervasive. My understanding is that almost a third of the Indian population lives below the poverty line, which in a country of nearly 1.1 billion people means that over 350 million people—more than the U.S. population—lack the basic food, clothing and shelter to survive.

And I believe it.

I can scarcely find the right words to describe the abject squalor I've witnessed. People living in wretched, horrible conditions, residing in what I can best describe as shanties constructed with whatever they can find, such as plywood and corrugated metal with roofs made of tarps held down by tires or large rocks, patched together to form a shelter but stretching any rational person's definition of a home.

But this *is* home for hundreds of millions of people, and it's a sobering, depressing sight. I see them everywhere. In open areas. On road sides and river banks. Under elevated freeways, and adjacent to five-star hotels.

Just today I saw a boy, probably no more than two or three years old, squatting on the side of the road not a block from our hotel, his pants around his ankles, urinating in the street.

How can anyone live this way? I think. And then my thoughts turn to what I have and I'm very thankful.

Which brings me back to the mother and child. I could've done something for her, but I didn't. It would've been easy to roll down my window and hand her some money, but I chose not to. It's not the first time I've turned away a beggar and it won't be the last. Bothered by the intrusion, it's easy to brush them off with a disgusted wave of your hand, forgotten by the time you arrive at your spacious home, park your SUV in your two car garage, sit on your couch and turn on your big screen high definition TV.

I'm not saying we should always give to beggars when approached. I'd be insincere if I said this experience has changed me and I'll forever reach into my pocket and make a handout when asked. No, my point is more fundamental. We live in a culture that is so self-absorbed and 'me'-focused that I'm afraid we've lost a vital quality.

Humility.

Despite the wretched conditions and seemingly hopeless prospects, I haven't found the Indian people to be angry at the world, wallowing in their entitlement. They are gracious people making the best with what they have, which is more than I can say for those of us in the Western world, myself included.

So I give thanks for my blessings, for humility despite the cultural influences to the contrary, for a more giving spirit, and especially for those in need. Maybe next time I'll be more giving and forgiving. Maybe next time I'll be more humble and less judgmental.

Maybe next time the image of a desperate woman's tears trickling down the car window won't be burned into my conscience.

I may be blessed by worldly standards, but this woman was blessed by other standards, a blessing that will outlast what this world has to offer.

Day 5—Delhi

Well, I have hot water after all.

It's in the bathtub.

I turned on the bathwater to wash my hair before breakfast, idly sitting on the side of tub while I waited for the water to become lukewarm. After a minute or so, I mindlessly reached my hand under the tap and drew it back immediately; the water scalded my fingers.

I've enjoyed the hot water. Why the tub has hot water while the sink and shower only a few feet away don't is beyond me. But I'm not looking this gift horse in the mouth. I'm shaving and taking hot baths in the tub until further notice.

The day began early, at 4:15 a.m., as Gopal, our host, Anuj (sounds like ah-NOOGE), and I were scheduled for a 7:00 a.m. flight to Delhi. Four sales calls were on the agenda, two with companies I recognized (Williams-Sonoma and Reebok).

Gopal and I met Anuj in the hotel lobby at 5:45 a.m., where the concierge hailed a taxi for the 10-15 minute ride to the domestic airport. There are two airports in Mumbai, one serving domestic markets in India and the other international destinations.

We flew Jet Airways, one of India's biggest passenger airlines and, gauging by the long lines we encountered at the main terminal, one of its most popular as well.

After passing through the requisite security checkpoints, we walked a short distance to the gate, where an agent accepted my boarding pass with a smile and a friendly, "Good morning, sir."

At the domestic airport—named Santa Cruz Airport (a strangely Hispanic-sounding name in a nation far removed from Spanish influence)—passengers don't walk jetways to board their flights. Instead, we walked through a door and exited the terminal to the tarmac outside, where we waited for a bus to shuttle us to our plane, which could be boarded at either end by climbing stairs-on-a-truck.

Despite the early hour, our flight was full and I had a middle seat in economy class, not my ideal seat location given my height but I made do. For your information: the cost of the ticket was 18,000 rupees, or about $400.

Beforehand, Gopal had prepped me that service on domestic Indian carriers is far superior to U.S. carriers, not that much is required to exceed service in America. While we waited for the plane to taxi to the runway—I didn't know yet how long that wait would be—the cabin crew cheerfully passed out newspapers, juice and bottled water, and tightly-rolled hand towels, cool and slightly damp, which I used to wipe away the last vestiges of morning lethargy.

The smooth sounds of jazz wafted from the overhead speakers, which brightened my mood considerably. I recognized many of the tunes, and if I closed my eyes, I could have easily been at home listening to my favorite jazz station rather than sitting on an idling airplane in a foreign land halfway around the world. Smooth jazz is one of my favorite musical genres (along with 80's music) and I can listen to its toe-tapping percussion, playful piano chords, and soothing saxophone sounds for hours. Frankly, you can keep today's pop, hip hop, head-banging, bass-thumping noise.

I'll take smooth jazz every day and twice on Sunday.

A disabled plane on the main runway delayed our departure for over two hours, most of which we spent sitting on the plane. I passed the time writing today's journal entry and working an addictive sudoku puzzle.

Gopal and I have had some interesting discussions about religion the past few days, driven primarily by my own curiosity about Hinduism. It's long been a curiosity of mine how there can be so many religions in the world. The followers of each are so staunchly—and perhaps stubbornly—supportive of their own beliefs that it's become an "I'm right and you're wrong" proposition. I can't say that I'm any closer to understanding Hinduism any more than I am to, say, quantum physics, but it hasn't stopped me from asking questions, and Gopal's patience and insight has been much appreciated.

To give you the Cliff's Notes version of what I've learned, followers of Hinduism believe in one god, but that god takes many forms, each of which may be worshiped.

My first reaction is to discount it based on pre-conceived beliefs, but I've tried to be respectful by not offering commentary. It's my opinion that there are too many people in the world who try to impose their religious will upon others, wasting time and energy to "save" people when what they should really be doing is listening.

At any rate, I've tried to keep an open mind and listen to Gopal's explanations and descriptions, though it's not easy when viewing it through a Western lens ingrained in the heart of a man who's been largely indifferent in matters of diversity.

I've learned a lot from Gopal and my other international co-workers. I believe that Americans are so convinced—overtly or not—that we are the best country in the world that this presumptuous and condescending attitude has spilled over into other perspectives—athletic, political, corporate and religious, to name a few—and it distorts our world view of not just nations but, more importantly, of people.

I'm pretty much set in my ways and I have a lot to learn, so I'm not suggesting that I've had a cultural or religious conversion. None of us change overnight. Yet I'm aware that the extent of my cultural exposure has been limited for the better part of my life and I could use a healthy dose of diversity and differing world views, if for no other reason than to make me a well-rounded person, less of a square peg in a world full of round holes, but I digress.

As I mentioned, we were two hours delayed in departing Mumbai, which caused a serious reshuffling of our agenda. We conducted only two of the planned three sales calls, which worked out well because we saw a bit more of the city than we would have otherwise, and Delhi is a beautiful city.

If one was to judge India by Mumbai alone, the experience would be far less impressive and probably negative, what with the horrendous traffic, choking smog, depressing poverty, and big city claustrophobia overshadowing some of the city's finer points. Delhi, by contrast, is the nation's capital and far more impressive a city.

Centrally located in northern India, Delhi is more spread out, allowing for more open green spaces, with better roads and developing infrastructure that has fostered a thriving, growing metropolis.

The highlight of the day was my first "real" Indian meal. Our party of four patronized a restaurant in south Delhi called Punjabi.

I asked Gopal for help in reading the menu but he assured me that we would order several entrees and share them. We ordered four items, all but one was vegetarian. After we placed the order, the waiter brought us a basket of bread.

The bread—called papad—looked like a small tortilla but was crispy like a cracker. They are baked with lots of pepper—too much, if you asked me—and despite all the water I drank I couldn't shake the strong aftertaste until our food arrived.

The non-vegetarian dish we ate—murg malai kabab—was cream grilled chicken on a kabob. Two of the vegetarian items were cheese dishes—paneer makani (cottage cheese gravy) and panroy tikka (grilled cottage cheese)—and the third was something called dal makhani, or lentil curry buttered. We shared between the four of us a large basket of naan, or tortilla-sized soft bread.

I eagerly dug in with knife and fork, thoroughly enjoying the mildly-spiced dishes, when Gopal asked if I wanted any bread. I said that I didn't, but I misunderstood.

What he said was that I needed to *use* my bread. Looking around the table, I then noticed my colleagues eating with their fingers, using the naan to pinch portions of, say, the lentil curry before eating it.

I smiled sheepishly and said something corny like, "Well, who am I not to eat with my fingers?" So I set aside my utensils and joined them. Following the meal, the waiter brought each of us a fingerbowl of hot water to wash away the food particles.

I really enjoyed the meal, and tomorrow promises another dining experience, as Anuj plans to take us to an Indian-Chinese restaurant in Mumbai that is well regarded.

There isn't much to report about the rest of my day, though I did have a 'dumb American' moment at our second sales call.

Midway through the meeting, nature called—the, ahem, sit-down variety. I excused myself to use the toilet. After a few minutes, I finished my business but couldn't find the flusher. It was neither on the front nor on either side. No pedal at the bottom either.

I was stumped.

Oh, great, I thought. The next person is going to come in here and find a treasure awaiting them and remember that the last person seen entering the bathroom was the tall white guy from America.

I felt panicky, and gave the toilet the once-over at least three times. I finally resolved to lift the lid and release the bowl from the inside. I grabbed a knob atop the tank and lifted it, and suddenly the toilet flushed. The knob was the flusher. All I had to do was pull it up and, voila!

Whew! Another crisis averted!

Just two more days to go before I go home and I can't wait! I miss Lana and the boys terribly; every time I see a child I think of them and long to be home.

One person I met this week told me that some people who come here like it so much that they want to stay, finding it difficult to board their flight home.

I'm 100% sure I won't have that problem.

Day 6—Light at the End of the Tunnel

Dateline: Mumbai, India
Date: 10/14/05 (or, as it's written in India, 14/10/05)
Today's top news story . . . .
I WANT TO GO HOME!!!!!!!!!!!!!

Not to minimize my India experience, which I'll remember for a long time, but I'm mentally and physically tired. I want to see my family, sleep in my bed, eat American food, sit in my recliner, breathe clean air, watch the baseball playoffs, read an American newspaper, and take a hot shower.

Everything I did Friday—the sales call, the meetings, lunch at an Indian-Chinese restaurant (which I didn't like very much)—competed with distracting thoughts of home. No disrespect to this fine country, but India has officially lost its luster.

I'm tired of sitting in the back seat of cramped cars with no seat belt. I'm tired of eating hotel food, not that it's bad but it just isn't what I want anymore. I'm tired of taking baths and shaving in the bathtub because it's the only place to get hot water. I'm tired of missing the boys' baseball and soccer games. I'm tired of thinking so hard about the little things, like which way to look when crossing the street or whether I should accept a glass of water for fear of contracting typhoid or hepatitis.

I'm tired of my life this past week, only work and sleep in a strange place so far from home. I respect people who travel for business on a regular basis, living out of suitcases in hotels, eating restaurant and fast food, flying hundreds, if not thousands, of miles from home, and they probably earn a good living doing so. But there's no amount of money that could convince me to live like this. It absolutely isn't worth it.

The price to pay—being away from family—is not worth the extra income or the travel to exciting places, for the excitement wears off quickly and I would imagine the rigors of business travel wears down even the strongest person. Time spent with family is just too important, but that's my opinion. It's also my choice, and we all know that our priorities define our choices.

So I guess you can tell I'm feeling a little frustrated today. Part of it is because I want to be home. Another part is the work. I feel that

I haven't added much value—professionally speaking. I've sat quietly in meetings, taking copious notes, adding little to the discussions. Having recently been assigned to the team conducting this analysis, my knowledge of the project and the market has been limited. But Gopal's extensive market knowledge and consulting strengths have carried me on this trip, and for that I am thankful.

Consulting isn't one of my strengths—nor is it one of my interests—and I'll probably add more value when I can utilize my storytelling and writing skills when we prepare the written analysis and presentation. So, I took solace in the light at the end of the tunnel, my departure growing closer by the minute.

As I write this, I'm sitting alone in my hotel room, a movie on TV (The Day After Tomorrow), eating Swiss chocolates for dinner. I could've had a more sustaining—and healthier—meal, but I declined Gopal's offer for dinner after our final meeting of the day. I felt bad for turning him down but I needed to unwind and be alone. I told him it was nothing personal and he said he understood, but I hope I didn't offend him. We've been together all week, it's been a long day and a long week and I needed to separate myself from the work and the people. I hope he meant it when he said he understood.

This solitude has given me some time to reflect on miscellaneous observations I've made this week.

First, few people in India are, to put it bluntly, fat. I think it's pretty well documented the large percentage of Americans who are overweight. Here, you don't see them very often. The food portions here are smaller and healthier, so it doesn't surprise me that most Indians aren't overweight.

While we're on the topic of food, it's also struck me that I seem to always be the last one to finish eating. Maybe it's because Indians eat fast, or maybe it's because I have a lot of my grandfather in me. It's probably a little of both.

Third, people here smoke like nobody's business. It wouldn't surprise me if Mumbai's pollution is partially caused by the sheer volume of cigarette consumption. There are hundreds of street vendors selling cigarettes; you can't drive a block without seeing someone peddling them. Indians love their smokes.

Fourth, ice isn't served in drinks. I first noticed this soon when my new workgroup took me out for a welcome-to-the-group lunch.

Everyone ordered water but my Indian coworkers ordered theirs without ice. Now I know why.

Order a Coke in Mumbai, it comes without ice. Order a McDonald's combo meal, the drink comes without ice. How about a glass of water before dinner? No ice. I'm not sure why this is. Maybe it has something to do with the water-borne disease threat, but I suspect it's more a cultural trait than anything.

Fifth, people here have trouble pronouncing the letter 'v'. For example, the word 'value' is pronounced 'walue'. I've wanted to ask Gopal about it, but decided it was an insensitive question. Anyhow, I'm just guessing, but the letter 'v' must somehow conflict linguistically with their native languages.

Well, it's getting late and I'm going to sign off, lie on the bed, and watch the movie. Gopal is leaving for his hometown of Chennai (aka Madras) early in the morning, so I have the entire day to myself while I wait for my departing flight, which leaves Mumbai about 1:00 a.m. Sunday morning.

Day 7-8—Going Home

Home again, home again. Jiggetty Jig.

I remember as a child when my family returned home from somewhere, usually a long vacation, my dad steered the car into our garage and said, "Home again, home again," and my brother, Rich, and I completed the sentence with an enthusiastic "Jiggetty jig." It always signaled the end of a journey, a welcome return home.

Now, I do the same with my two sons, though they sometimes respond with a "jiggetty jog", but I don't mind. Anyway, when I pulled into the garage this evening, honking the horn to announce my arrival, the boys threw open the doors to the minivan (they'd just arrived home from Will's coach-pitch baseball game), shrieking "Daddy" as they jumped out of the car. Through the open car window, I yelled, "Home again, home again," and they screamed "jiggety jig" as they threw their arms around me, giving me hugs so tight that I wanted to bottle them forever.

Thus ended a long two days that began in Mumbai and ended in the suburbs of Memphis. Not long ago, world travel would've been a weeks-long experience. Today, it can be yours for a few thousand dollars and a day and a half.

Amazing thing, technology!

I slept in Saturday morning, waking casually, catching the end of the Angels-White Sox game on TV before descending the lift to the hotel spa, where I spent several hours, first a massage, followed by a half-hour on the treadmill, then time in the Jacuzzi.

I've mentioned several times about the excellent service the hotel staff provides, and they take it to a new level in the spa.

The massage room looks much the same as any other: dimmed lights, easy listening music playing in the background (it sounded like cheesy love scene music from a Danielle Steele made-for-TV movie), and pleasant aroma filling the room. My masseuse—a short, petite female, dark hair pulled back in a ponytail—welcomed me with a friendly "Good morning, sir" (people respectfully say 'sir' and 'ma'am' a lot, I've noticed). From a cabinet behind her, she opened a drawer and, turning around, handed me something that looked like a cheap Kleenex.

"Your panty, sir?"

She dropped it in my palm and gestured behind me to where I should change out my clothes and don the panty. I held it between my fingers and calculated it might fit my kids just fine but, on me, it would serve as anal floss.

She left the room and I put on the panty. Fortunately, it was made of a paper-like material, so I made a few strategic tears to ease pressure on the sensitive areas. Anyway, it was an excellent massage, very relaxing, and when it was over I couldn't get that Ferris Buehler song out of my head. You know what I'm talking about? The tune with the booming, Barry White-like bass voice.

"Oohhhhhh, yeaaaaaahhhhhhh." (BOW! BOW! chicka chick-ahhhhhh)

After the massage, I ran for half an hour on the treadmill, the massage oils still adhering to my skin. I was the best smelling jogger in the house.

After the run, I sat in the Jacuzzi a while. Let me tell you how classy the spa was. Leading up the stairs to the Jacuzzi were about a half dozen folded towels, terrycloth stepping stones to prevent slipping on the marble floors. I sat in the Jacuzzi for maybe ten minutes, which was all I could take because the water was too hot to tolerate much longer. At one end of the Jacuzzi sat a television set. I found the remote and turned the TV to the Hallmark channel, where I watched a rerun of 'Mad About You'.

Following the hot tub, I hit the showers and took my first hot shower in a week. This wasn't just any shower. Round and lined with one inch brown tiles, the shower looked different than any I'd seen before. Looking up, a dinner plate-sized shower head descended from the ceiling and sent a relaxing spray of water straight down on my head and shoulders. Mounted on the walls around me, three vertical pipes each contained four regular shower heads, aimed horizontally. It took me a while to figure out the control knobs, but once deciphered, it was like taking a Jacuzzi shower, a 3-D hydro massage with water from above and three sides.

I liked it so much I returned for a second shower in the evening.

I spent all day in the hotel. Check-out time was supposed to be 12:00 noon Saturday but my flight wouldn't leave until 13 hours later. Frankly, I wasn't excited about spending a half-day in Mumbai by myself, so I extended my hotel stay, which would allow me to enjoy my last day within the comfy confines of the Hyatt.

I skipped breakfast and ate a hearty lunch, my favorite item being aloo pakoda, best described as a deep fried potato chip but spicier and thicker.

I acted the sloth for the rest of the day: surfing the Internet, Watching bad movies (If you come across the movie 'Money Train' starring Woody Harrelson and Wesley Snipes, please resist the urge to watch), eating the rest of my Swiss chocolate, and packing my suitcase.

<Yawn>.

I left the hotel around 10:30 p.m. for a five-minute drive to the international airport. I probably could've stayed at the hotel longer but I'd grown too stir crazy to spend another minute in the hotel.

My flight departed Mumbai about 1:00 a.m. Despite the overwhelming urge to take an afternoon nap, I'd forced myself to stay awake all day and, for once, had little trouble sleeping on the plane. I fell asleep not long after take-off and when I awoke somewhere over Turkey, I was surprised to learn I'd slept almost six hours.

With three hours to kill before landing in Amsterdam, I read a book (a new Stephen King pulp fiction murder mystery called "The Colorado Kid"), ate breakfast (nothing fancy), and watched a movie ('Mr. and Mrs. Smith' with Angelina Jolie and Brad Pitt), though the picture kept blacking out and I missed the ending, turning it off in frustration from the many interruptions.

I had a 7-hour layover in Amsterdam. When I first departed the U.S., I entertained the idea of taking a taxi into the city to see the sites, but we landed before sunrise and I remained tired from the long flight. It wasn't until later when I roamed the airport and found a kiosk selling guided tours of Amsterdam did I rethink my decision, but by then it was too late. So I spent most of the layover in the KLM Crown Lounge, where the coolest amenity was the self-service mixed drinks.

The many liquor bottles were mounted upside down on a wall. Let's say you wanted a rum and coke. You'd take a glass and push it against a lever like on a fountain drink machine and the rum would flow from the bottle.

After spending hours in the lounge, I roamed the airport, ducking in and out of stores, buying another box of Swiss chocolates, browsing books and magazines, some of them risqué, witnessing how Europeans are more open about their sexuality than Americans.

I'm casually walking through a newsstand, browsing book titles. I stopped at a rack of John Grisham novels, turning them over to see which ones I haven't read. Something in my peripheral vision catches my attention. Turning to my right toward the magazine stand, I saw a section of adult magazines, not a few tucked away on the top row, wrapped in plastic and strategically covered like those in American bookstores, but a whole section of them, uncovered, row upon row of 40 DD's exposed for the world to see.

So I about-faced and checked out the electronics, which were adjacent to the bookstore. After browsing for a few minutes, I exited the store, which took me through the DVD section, which contained row upon row of adult titles.

I decided then it was time to find my gate, take a seat, read, and await boarding.

The return flight seemed interminable. I constantly watched the clock, knowing I was getting closer to home every second. I watched a few movies and napped a little, but only when the wheels touched the ground did I finally sigh in relief.

Final thoughts about India: it's an interesting place, its people gracious and friendly, its food spicy but satisfying, a place with potential though not without serious problems. Would I go back? Maybe, but there are other places—many places—I'd choose to visit first.

I'm home now, sitting at the computer in my office. The boys are in bed, wearing eye shades I gave them from my amenity kits. They're supposed to be asleep but I can hear them chatting away like they do most nights. Lana and I just watched the latest episode of *Desperate Housewives*, and I have a little catching up to do since I missed last week's show. In the hours since I arrived, I read the Sunday paper, caught up on the ball scores (Cardinals lost again), and ate a wonderfully fattening dinner of Wal-mart fried chicken and mashed potatoes, followed by a special dessert of chocolate Moose Tracks ice cream to celebrate my return.

Ah, it's good to be home.

Which reminds me of a famous quote by novelist Tom Wolfe, who once wrote, "You can't go home again."

Well, you can.

I did.

And it feels so good!

The author standing in front of Mumbai's Gateway of India, akin to the Statue of Liberty in New York.

The author posing in Mumbai's Hanging Gardens with Marine Drive—aka the 'Queen's Necklace'—in the background.

Author's Note

I hope you've enjoyed these writings, letting you share in my travel experiences, giving you a glimpse into my head and my heart (now I know what it feels like to blog). What I intended to be a travel journal developed into something deeper and more personal. I intended not to write a memoir but instead to inform (and, hopefully, entertain) select family and friends through daily emails detailing my adventures. Being an introvert and guarded about many things, I found it hard at times to be so revealing, but, in retrospect, it's been a cathartic exercise, helping me deal with my longing for home.

I'm very grateful to my employer (FedEx) for sending me overseas and for years of content employment. I'm also thankful for my travel companions (Gopal Narasimhan and Ann Parbery) for their fellowship, friendship, and for tolerating my constant musings.

Thanks also to my wife and sons for your love and support. I wouldn't be the person I am today without it.

About The Author

JEFF MARTINDALE is the author of three books: *An Accidental Globetrotter*, a humorous memoir of his international travels, *Going to the Beach*, a children's book for young readers, and *Random Thoughts*, a collection of short stories and essays. He lives in Collierville, Tennessee with his wife and two sons.